BUSES

ALEXANDERS

REMEMBERED

Vol. 2. 1961 - 1985

20 years of Leyland bus operation is evident in this scene at Glasgow's Buchanan Street bus station with Kilsyth's Albion Lowlander MRE13, really a Leyland with Albion badges, about to set off for Falkirk and in the background TS8 Special P641, new in 1940, on a local service to Annathill. The crew are concerned with the time by the looks of it, but despite being firmly in the Midland era one could be forgiven for thinking that the 'empire' still ruled.

Allan T. Condie

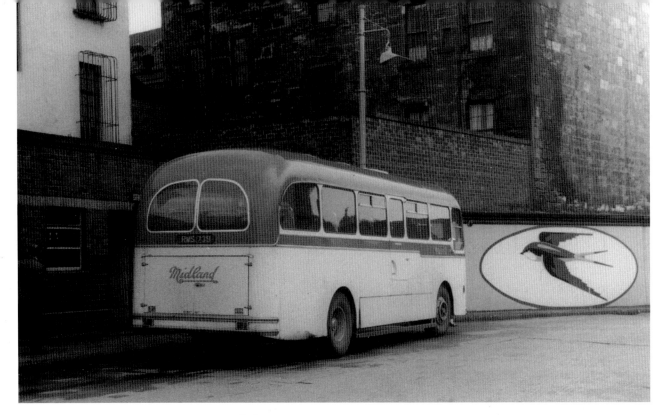

Contents

ISBN 1 85638 017 3 Hardback   ISBN 1 85638 018 1 Paperback

Design, Layout and editing by Allan T. Condie
Typesetting and reproduction by Rivers Media Services
Printed in England.

Allan T. Condie Publications, 40 Main Street, Carlton, NUNEATON CV13 ORG. Tel./Fax 01455-290389.

Introduction

One of the joys of the past six months or so have been the constant stream of letters of enthusiasm and approval of "Alexanders Buses Remembered Vol. 1." Over the past 18 years I have written nearly 100 books and that one book has created more interest than anything else. Indeed we now have a fledgling "Alexander Study Group" as a result. And so we move on into the sixties with this book.

The second volume of the Alexander story has for me, at least, proved a little more difficult to grasp. The split-up of the empire into three in 1961 took away some of the aura of the organisation, and as the personal interest seemed to wane as more modern vehicles replaced old friends one could be forgiven for being less observant as to what went on, especially once the swinging sixties had passed into history. But there were excitements; a Sunday trip in 1962 to travel on the new Bristol Lodekka FLFs, and the sight of the first Y type outside Perth depot. Trips to Blairgowrie on the 'yellow' buses and St. Andrews on the 'red' ones kept one in touch.

Not only that, but like so many others the necessity of bus travel ended when one was able to drive, and eventually buy one's own car. The blue buses of Midland still passed our house in Perth however, and one was able to note the arrival of the VRs and their short stay in the North, Fleetlines, Vikings, Nationals and finally Ailsas. 1985 and my move away from Scotland saw the end of 'Midland' and really the three 'Empire States' as I knew them, but one last event which was really to revive my interest in buses was the loan of two of Clydeside's Routemasters for trials in Perth in the October of that year. My final thought is one of riding on the front of the top deck of one of those vehicles from Scone into Perth. Memories of earlier ex London vehicles came flooding back and started a journey into the past which has resulted in this series of books.

Insofar as Alexanders is concerned, it is not intended to take the story of successor Companies any further, but we will be looking back at sometime in the future, I hope, to the formative period before 1945. The next Alexander treatise will be one on Alexander bodywork from 1945-60. "But what about other members of the SMT group?" many of you have asked - the answer is 'wait and see'. Tell your friends about our first two books, encourage them to buy and who knows - we may get round the lot in the fullness of time. But one final thought - our forthcoming Perthshire Buses Remembered will have a good slice of the Alexanders cake in it .

June 1997.   *Allan T. Condie*

Acknowledgements

Once again without so many friends to help this book would have been impossible to complete. Again I have been able to identify the sources of many of the photographs but I apologise if any are incorrectly attributed.

John Burnett, Gavin Booth, Ian Clapperton, Alastair Cruickshank, Alistair Douglas, Robert Grieves, Neil MacDonald, Ian MacGregor, Roy Marshall, Douglas Parker, Ray Simpson, Raymond Thom, Jim Thompson, Peter Walton, Brian Wright, and Geoff Wright have all helped in some way, and again I must thank so many who wrote with their own reminiscences after the appearance of the first volume.

Opposite: One part of the image created for the 'empire' still in use today is the Bluebird emblem. The largest example of same was once to be found on the wall at Buchanan Street Bus Station, Glasgow.

Country Connection 2. Alexanders (Midland) MNV8 makes the connection for Balloch operated by The Loch Lomond Bus Co's Ford at Drymen Village Green in February 1970. It is winter, in contrast to the same location in Vol. 1. taken some 10 years earlier.

The Alexanders Story from 1961

1- Three out of one!

As detailed in Vol. 1 of this series, Alexanders from 1949 had been part of the Scottish Group of Bus Companies whose State ownership was vested in the British Transport Commission. The Company had always been divided into three areas, Southern, based on Falkirk, Northern, based on Aberdeen, and Fife, based on Kirkcaldy, each with its own workshop facilities. As part of the desire to make smaller more manageable units within the group, from 15th May 1961 the Alexander empire was split into three companies taking over responsibility for each of the former areas.

There were a number of underlying reasons for this move. The 'golden age' of bus travel was over, and the two biggest factors which affected omnibus travel for leisure, television and the increase in the private car population were beginning to have effect. Admittedly, there were some gains due to the withdrawal of railway passenger services on some unremunerative routes, but the full effects of the Beeching cuts were yet to come. By taking management closer to the area of operations, it was argued that greater efficiency and cost savings would be achieved.

The largest fleet of over 900 vehicles went to Walter Alexander & Sons (Midland) Ltd., whose head office was located at Brown Street, Camelon. Into this Company was absorbed the activities of David Lawson of Kirkintilloch whose fleet ceased to maintain a separate identity.

With nearly 500 vehicles, Walter Alexander & Sons (Fife) Ltd. and with 450 vehicles, Walter Alexander & Sons (Northern) Ltd. were created by renaming existing British Transport Commission Companies whose activities had been taken over by other subsidiaries. Youngs Express Deliveries (BTC) Ltd became the Northern Company and Cowan & Co. (BTC) Ltd. became the Fife Company. These two firms had been road hauliers taken over with the nationalisation of road transport in 1948, and they became fully integrated into British Road Services (Scotland) from 1949.

The Fife Company had headquarters at Esplanade Kirkcaldy, and the Northern one at Gairn Terrace, Hardgate, Aberdeen.

The only outward signs of change could be ascertained when the legal lettering on the vehicles began to be altered; however fleetnames were also changed to show "& Sons (Midland) Ltd", "& Sons (Fife) Ltd", or "& Sons (Northern) Ltd"

below the "Alexander" portion. As ticket stocks ran out the names of the new Companies also appeared on these.

In 1962 however, it was announced that each of the Companies would have new liveries and fleetnames. The fleetnames were abbreviations to 'Midland', 'Fife' and 'Northern'. Whilst the Midland fleet retained their blue livery Northern adopted yellow and Fife Ayres red. This also spelt the end for Lawson's red and the dark red of Perth City and Kirkcaldy town service vehicles; the Fife red being a lighter shade however.

The balance of vehicles ordered by the former Company were split for delivery to the new subsidiaries for the rest of 1961 and part of 1962. In the first part of each photographic section of this book we shall look at vehicles transferred to the new Companies.

All three Companies remained vested in the British Transport Commission until 1969 when the Scottish Transport Group was set up to acquire ownership of the Scottish group of bus companies, the Caledonian Steam Packet Co. and subsequently David MacBrayne Ltd.

Over the following years economic and other pressures were to have a drastic effect on how bus services were run and the profitability of the Companies. The Scottish Transport Group's annual report on its inception in 1969 showed that Midland operated 952 vehicles, Fife 512 and Northern 509. By 1978 this had fallen to 690 for Midland. 416 for Fife and 398 for Northern. The first Alexander OMO operations started in 1959 from Pitlochry using a converted PS1 Leyland Tiger. The decline in passenger numbers and rising costs meant that the future lay in single manning, but the running costs of the vehicles concerned, high capacity single and double deck vehicles with front entrances, both in fuel and maintenance terms, rose sharply. For this reason few double deckers were added to the fleets in the early 1970s, the bias being towards high capacity single deckers. The unpopularity of the Bristol VRT resulted in the exchanges with NBC Companies for Lodekkas, and the Scottish Bus Group as a whole were responsible for aiding and abetting the development of the Volvo/Ailsa double decker and Seddon single deck vehicles.

The early 1970s were also a period of staff shortages, high wage demands and the inevitable industrial action resulted from this with major

4

disruption. Fife and Midland suffered badly from strike action by staff in 1970. Rising costs due to wage increases which could not be absorbed by fare increases were to a certain extent cushioned by the bus grant which originally set at 25% later halved the cost of replacement vehicles. Then the oil crisis of 1972/3, added to high inflation brought about further disruption with unofficial strike action in the latter part of 1974. As time passed a higher proportion of mileage operated was with OMO vehicles, the fact that the bus grant encouraged the purchase of this type of vehicle saw

a rapid decline in the use of front engined double deckers in the mid to late 1970s.

The National Bus Company in England & Wales had instigated a Market Analysis project (MAP) in the 1970s to investigate current traffic patterns and assess future needs for bus travellers. The Scottish Bus Group followed suit and SCOTMAP was instigated, major surveys being taken all over Scotland during 1979 and 1980 resulting in a major recasting of service patterns, timings and even routes.

Midland

Midland's operating area covered the central belt of Scotland, with its most northerly outposts at Pitlochry and Oban. The busiest routes were around Glasgow, where there had been some gains in the late fifties due to Glasgow Corporation withdrawing its tramway services outside the city boundary from 1956. Midland was also responsible for urban and suburban routes in Falkirk, Grangemouth, Larbert, Stirling, Alloa, and Perth. It wasn't long before activities in the north western outpost at Oban were strengthened with the acquisition of Duncan MacDougall of Oban in April 1962 who operated 7 vehicles, none of which was involved in the takeover. The increase in fleet size gave Oban depot its independence as it had always been an sub-depot of Stepps.

A familiar sight around Coatbridge were the red buses of Carmichael of Glenboig, often confusing to the unknowing due to the use of the 'Highland' fleet name. Carmichael succumbed in August 1966, and this takeover did involve the vehicles, not all of which were operated however. The rapidly expanding new town of Cumbernauld was to see the opening of its own depot in November

1967. David MacBrayne Ltd. had been jointly owned by the Transport Holding Company on behalf of the Secretary of State for Scotland and Coast Lines Ltd. The state acquired this 50% holding from Coast Lines in July 1969. David MacBrayne's coaching operations in Glasgow were transferred to Midland in October 1970 and 14 vehicles taken over and Oban depot and its 14 vehicles was transferred to Highland Omnibuses Ltd. MacBrayne's had operated extensive coach tours from Glasgow and these passed to Midland along with 18 vehicles. The rest of the MacBrayne bus services passed to Highland and Western SMT. An interesting 'paper' transfer was the ownership of the Paddle Steamer 'Maid of the Loch' to Midland in 1972; the Caledonian Steam Packet Co. continued to be responsible for its operation and upkeep however.

The 1970s saw rationalisation of unremunerative rural routes, and it came as a surprise after Midland had passed some services over to Yuills that Aberfeldy Motor Coaches, a long established operator in the area was taken over along with two Bedfords - both of which finished up at Crieff!

Fife

The Fife area covered the 'kingdom' but with through services to the North, South and West. One of the most important changes to service patterns involved the opening of the Forth Road Bridge on the 4th September 1964 and the Tay Road Bridge on the 18th of August 1966. Along with other group members service patterns were altered to take account of the considerable advantages found in operating services to Fife and the North from Edinburgh. Rail services to Tayport had been curtailed at Newport on Tay East due to bridge construction from 18th December 1967 and bus services adjusted accordingly, and the local rail service was withdrawn completely from 5th May 1969. But there were other reasons for the abandonment of rail services which diverted what traffic that

remained onto the buses, as other lines in Fife also became victims of the Beeching axe.

The old Fife area premises at Kirkcaldy became the base for operations and as a result of the adoption of the new red livery it was necessary for a time to fit "Town Service" boards to vehicles operating in Kirkcaldy.

Inevitably, several small operators were absorbed in the 1960s, these being Eastern Roadways of Anstruther in April 1965, none of whose four vehicles were operated, Niven of St. Andrews in October 1967 whose one Bedford lasted in the Fife fleet until 1972, and R. Drysdale & Sons of Cupar in December 1967 whose three vehicles were passed on to Highland Omnibuses.

Northern

The Northern Company inherited the least populated area of the three new entities, along with busy suburban services out of Aberdeen, and a network of other routes linking the North East's Capital with the coastal towns of Peterhead, Fraserburgh, Banff, and inland routes towards Elgin and finally Inverness. The area was also well endowed with local railways most of which fell to the Beeching axe leaving only the main Aberdeen-Inverness service via Inverurie, which had been in the past an important railway town with workshops belonging to the former Great North of Scotland Railway. Suburban railway services along the Dee valley to Ballater along with the fact that the direct route licence for a bus services was held by Strachan's Deeside Omnibus Services prevented expansion there until the railway passenger service was withdrawn on 28th February 1966. Prior to this date however, negotiations had commenced to take over Strachans and this took effect from May 1965, giving Alexanders (Northern) a monopoly on Deeside after the trains had finished.

There still existed a fairly strong independent presence in the North East of the region with Burnett of Mintlaw and Simpson of Rosehearty holding licences for local services in the Peterhead area as well as trunk routes into Aberdeen. Simpsons succumbed in December 1966 and Burnetts in January 1967. It is interesting to note that takeovers generally followed the withdrawal of railway services to a greater or lesser degree so that the British Transport Commission still ruled.

To the south of the region from 4th September 1967 the direct rail link from Stanley Junction through Forfar to Kinnaber Junction was withdrawn, and a replacement express bus service was instigated between Perth and Forfar. Mitchell of Luthermuir, an independent operating in the Montrose and Brechin area was taken over in October 1967 - another co-incidence?

Whilst the rail retrenchment brought some extra revenue, including that of parcel traffic, the main factor in improving economic prospects in the area came with the discovery of North Sea oil and gas. In the early 1970s there was scope for improvement in services, and this was reflected in the introduction of an Aberdeen-London coach service in 1973, which also involved connections with the Aberdeen-Glasgow service jointly operated by Midland and Northern. The Scottish connection with Corby in Northamptonshire saw another weekend express service begin in 1975 between there and Aberdeen in conjunction with Barton Transport Ltd.

Other growth areas in traffic in the Aberdeen area in the early 1970s saw the transfer of additional double deck vehicles from other members of the Scottish Bus Group.

Two important former Municipal operators in the shape of Tayside Regional Council and Grampian Regional Council operated in the Northern area, and it made economic sense to co-operate in certain areas of operation. The Tayway scheme came into operation in the Dundee area in 1980 and this involved co-operation with Tayside Regional Transport and British Rail. Whilst advertising matter and timetables carried the Tayway slogan this was not extended to the vehicles as was the case in Aberdeen when local services operated by Northern and Grampian Regional Transport were united under the *Grampian Scottish* banner and vehicles from the Northern fleet were repainted in green and cream with *Grampian Scottish* fleetnames.

Scottish Citylink

The deregulation of express services as a result of the 1980 transport act meant that operators could run express services of over 30 miles in length without the normal licensing procedures from the Traffic Commissioners. This brought a number of new operators into this field including the fledgling Stagecoach and in October 1983 the Scottish Bus Group launched a new corporate identity for this service under the *Citylink* banner, following trials with some coaches under the *Cityliner* banner. All the groups vehicles used on express services were finished in a striking two tone blue and yellow livery.

The end of the Alexander name

In 1978 the Scottish Bus Group introduced a new corporate identity with all fleetnames of the group ending in *Scottish* and the three former Alexander companies were *Fife Scottish, Midland Scottish and Northern Scottish* respectively. The fleetnames were split by the use of a saltaire symbol based on the Scottish flag. This was the beginning of the end for the three subsidiaries as from 1st March 1985 the three Companies were renamed *Fife Scottish Omnibuses Ltd., Midland Scottish Omnibuses Ltd., and Northern Scottish Omnibuses Ltd.* The Scottish Bus Group was to be further broken down into units which corresponded to the Regional Authorities in all regions except Strathclyde, where the breakdown was roughly in line with the districts in that Region. The result was 11 Companies and only Fife remained substantially the same as it was.

Midland Scottish lost 4 garages to Kelvin Scottish and three to Strathtay, and Northern lost five garages to Strathtay. What has happened since is outside the scope of this publication.

The Alexanders Fleets from 1961

As most of the orders for vehicles delivered in 1961 had been placed before the split-up it was noticeable that batches of vehicles appeared in full Alexanders blue livery and fleetnames, with only the legal lettering altered. One significant change took place however, and that involved registration marks. Fife vehicles were now licenced at Kirkcaldy and received SP and FG marks, whilst Northern vehicles were licenced in Aberdeen and received RS and RG marks. Midland continued as before.

On order at the time of the split were 25 Leyland Titan PD3A/3 chassis. These were completed with Alexander 67 seat lowbridge bodies. 18 went to Midland and 7 to Northern, the latter receiving RS registrations. These were the only vehicles involved in any break-up of orders, the 1961 Tiger Cubs and Reliances all went to Midland.

Midland

The 1961 deliveries to Midland after the split involved 5 Reliances, and one Tiger Cub, although the vehicles involved had been completed earlier and were in store. A further 19 Tiger Cubs, and 18 PD3s were also delivered during the ensuing three months as were the balance of Lodekkas accounting for 8 vehicles including the last LD6G, RD160 which also had the distinction of being the last vehicle delivered in Perth City red livery.

In 1962 the first 12 Bristol FLFs arrived and were all allocated to Perth. There were also 19 Tiger Cubs fitted with a new style of Alexander body based on the then current pattern used for BET companies but with normal Alexander pattern front ends. Four Bedford VAS1s also arrived, three with coach bodies and one with bus body, all by Duple. There was also a transfer of stock from Northern involving four prewar Titans and 9 ex Sutherland Daimlers. The vehicles acquired from McDougall in Oban were quickly disposed of.

1963 saw the arrival of the first Albion Lowlanders along with more Reliances and Tiger Cubs, and these were the first single deckers with Alexander Y type bodies. There were another 10 70 seat Lodekkas, and finally 6 Bedford VAS1 coaches. The following year saw the last of the 'new' Lodekkas, and the first of the 36' long Leyland Leopards with Alexander Y type bodies, there were coach and bus versions of these, but a small batch of 30' long Tiger Cubs proved to be the last of this type delivered new.

The shape of things to come in the form of a single Albion Viking was seen at various garages during 1964 and this front engined vehicle had been exhibited at the 1963 Scottish Motor Show on the Albion stand. When 10 Vikings arrived in 1965 however they were of the rear engined VK43L type. Indeed 1965 was the year of the single decker with 52 Leyland leopards arriving also - these were 49 seaters.

1966 was a lean year indeed with only six more Albion Vikings delivered. The milestone of 1967 if one could call it that was the arrival of 45 Daimler Fleetlines, the balance of that year's orders being Albion Viking buses and Bedford VAM coaches, indeed more Fleetlines and Vikings were all that came in 1968.

1969 ended the Viking invasion with just one final example arriving and only eight Leyland Leopards.

The Bristol VRT appeared on the scene in 1970, these accounting for 15 units, along with more Fleetlines including the first with ECW bodies, more Leopards, some 'wee' Bedfords for extended tours work, and a first in the shape of 19 Bristol LH chassis which were bodied by Alexander.

Only four Fleetlines arrived in 1971, underlining the group's dislike of this type and the new order in the shape of four Leopards with 53 seat bus bodies. There were also another 14 Bristol LH coaches. This was also the year in which the Bristol VRTs were despatched south in exchange for 15 FLF6G Lodekkas.

There was a large intake of single deckers in 1972, with 40 Leyland Leopards and 8 more Bristol LHs arriving; 37 more Leopards came in 1973 but only four Fleetlines. Again the majority of the single deckers were 53 seat buses with a few 45 and 49 seaters also. 1974 saw a change to Ford for the lightweight single deck chassis both with Duple and Alexander bodies, but there were still more Leopards and that pattern was to continue through 1975, with 21 more Fleetlines arriving in 1976 with more Fords.

1977 saw the Ailsas arrive, fourteen of them - these being the first full height double deckers purchased new since RB102/3 of 1950. With the closure of many railway lines they could be used more effectively than in earlier days due to the demolition of a number of low bridges, but Perth became a natural home for some.

The balance of 1977 deliveries consisted of more Fords and Leopards, a pattern which was repeated in 1978 when no double deckers were received at all.

The next innovation was the arrival of 15 Leyland Nationals at the end of 1978; was this new concept to be the answer for Midland's future orders? Well no! Certainly another 22, this time of the National 2 type arrived at the beginning and end of 1980, but that year also saw more Leopards and the last of the Fleetlines bringing the grand total of this type operated to 170. A prototype Olympian also joined the fleet but this passed to Northern by the summer after being tried by other SBG group members. Back to 1979 however, when the First Metrobuses arrived, three of them, plus 43 Leopards, both buses and coaches and 20 Fleetlines.

More Tigers and Metrobuses were on hand for 1981 and 1982, but by 1983 Leyland's new Tiger chassis had replaced the Leopard and this was chosen for all future single deck deliveries until 1985 with the Metrobus now the choice for double deckers.

Fife

Fife's 1961 deliveries consisted of what was in effect the balance of the 1960 orders for LD6G Lodekkas, Fife receiving 13; the first vehicles delivered to the new company also having Stirlingshire registrations, these being 11 Tiger Cubs.

Fife took more Lodekkas in 1962, but these were 13 FLF6G models. The surprise of the year however was the arrival of 12 AEC Reliances, the first AEC's in the Fife fleet. There were also 4 Bedford VAS1s, three coaches and a bus, all with Duple bodies. More Reliances arrived in 1963 and 1964; the first 7 Albion Lowlanders in 1963 and Fife reverted to rear entrance 27' Lodekkas, receiving 20 in 1963 and 14 in 1964, along with a solitary Bedford VAS1 coach.

Only 12 new vehicles, Albion Vikings came in 1965, but the Lowlander fleet was enlarged with the arrival of 18 units from Central SMT. 1966 was an all single deck year for new deliveries, these being 13 Vikings and 14 Reliances, these of course having the Alexander Y type body. Central supplied two Titan PD2s and two Guy Arab IIIs, and from Western came more Lowlanders, bringing the number in the Fife fleet up to 34.

More Albion Vikings were purchased in 1967, along with the last of the Lodekkas which were FLF6Gs, but of the longer variety seating 75; there were 18 of these. Another 5 Lowlanders came from Western together with 2 other odd double deckers, a PD1 and a Guy Arab.

It will be remembered that the Fife area had received all 20 Bristol LS saloons new in 1955 and 12 Bristol RE buses with ECW 53 seat bus bodies continued that tradition when they arrived in 1968 along with the first 20 Fleetlines. 1970 saw delivery of another 14 Fleetlines and Fife's first Leopards, 13 of them with 49 coach seats. 1971 was the year of the Fleetline with another 48, a mix of Alexander, Northern Counties and ECW bodies were evident.

The distaste for rear engined double deckers saw only one Fleetline delivered over the next three years, the Leyland Leopard accounting for the rest of the new vehicles; there were 62 in service by May 1974, The first 2 Fords arrived later that year, with the balance of that order making up most of the single deck deliveries in 1975. Three Leopards were also delivered in that year, being long distance coaches with toilets for the new direct services to London from 'the Kingdom', the service having been started with three borrowed coaches from Scottish Omnibuses. It was hoped that double decker troubles would be 'left behind' with 40 Volvo Ailsas entering service; vehicle shortages however saw the acquisition of some ex Edinburgh PD2s which were not operated but donated their engines to ailing Lowlanders.

There were no new deliveries in 1976; 1977 saw another six Ailsas and 7 Leyland Leopard buses. More Leopards arrived in 1978, and Fife's first 13 Leyland Nationals. 1979 saw the last of the true Ailsas, and more Leyland Nationals, this time of the National 2 variety. 1980 to 83 saw Leyland Leopards predominate, although there were another 10 National 2s. From 1983 the Leopards lost their spots and became Tigers of which 11 had been received by the end of 1984, the balance of 1983 deliveries being 10 Leyland Olympians and 20 Volvo double deckers arrived in 1984 and 1985, two of these being seated as coaches.

Northern

There was only one delivery to the northern area in 1961 before the split and that was Reliance AC200. The seven PD3s mentioned earlier arrived between August and October and were the first vehicles to receive Aberdeen registrations. 1962 saw the continuance of an AEC preference with

18 Reliances, these having the latest style of Alexander body derived from those then currently being supplied to English BET group companies but with the standard Alexander pattern front end. There were also four small Bedford VAS1s, three coaches and a bus, all with Duple bodies.

Two Albion Lowlanders invaded the north-east in 1963, and another 21 Reliances, this time with the new Y type body, indeed 1964 accounted for another 18 of the same along with one more Bedford coach. 1965 saw the first Leylands since the split, and these were Northern's first 36 footers which accounted for just 4 units of the Leopard variety with 49 seat coach bodies. The Albion Viking also made its debut in 1965 with the first 15 and added to that was the takeover of 12 vehicles from Strachans of Ballater of which only two survived that year. More double deckers arrived but these were three Lowlanders from Western SMT.

There were no new vehicles for 1966 but the 31 strong fleet of Simpsons of Rosehearty was absorbed in December of that year. Some of the Fords and Bedfords so acquired were passed on to Highland; the last ex-Simpson vehicle going in 1976.

The other major independent in the north-east, Burnett of Mintlaw was taken over on 9th January 1967 and this involved 14 vehicles, again the last of these were operated until 1976. It was an all single deck year for new vehicles with no fewer than 35 Albion Vikings and another 6 Leyland Leopards. One unusual purchase was an Austin Princess car which was used on a new service between Dundee and Edinburgh's Turnhouse airport via the newly opened Tay Road Bridge and the Forth Road Bridge. At the end of the year the 11 strong fleet of Mitchells of Luthermuir was acquired; the last of the ex Mitchell vehicles survived until 1972.

Bedfords, Albions and Leylands predominated in 1968, but there were some differences. In addition to three VAS1 29 seat coaches there were two 35 seat buses on VAM70 chassis. All had Duple bodies, but the Alexander Y type body was to be found on 13 more Albion Vikings and 6 Leyland Leopards, the last mentioned being 53 seat buses; the first of this type with Northern. In 1969 there were a further 20 Vikings bringing the total supplied to Northern to date to 83. Second-hand acquisitions in 1970 accounted for 6 AEC Reliances from Scottish Omnibuses.

The seventies dawned with two more cars added to the fleet; these were Ford Dorchester II conversions of the Ford Granada. More Duple bodied Bedfords arrived in the shape of 4 VAM70s with 45 seat bus bodies and further Vikings brought the grand total to 88. Two more AEC Reliances arrived from Highland Omnibuses and 18 Leyland PD2 double deckers dating from 1955-56 came from Western SMT, to help with the increased traffic associated with the North Sea oil boom in Aberdeen.

All 1971 bus deliveries were single deckers with Alexander 53 seat bodies, there being 15 Fords on R226 chassis bodied by Alexander and another 13 Leopards. Another Ford Dorchester was purchased. More used double deckers, 13 in all, from Western SMT. 1972 was an all Ford year with two R1014s bodied by Duple as 45 seaters and the other 5 bodied by Alexander as 41 seaters. The other 15 were 53 seat buses on R1114 chassis. Another car, this time a Zodiac, was acquired. Six Albion Vikings from Scottish Omnibuses also found new homes with Northern, as received these were 34 seat coaches and were soon reseated as either 44 seat buses or 38 seat coaches.

1973 and 1974 saw the arrival of more Fords, 43 in all, with the 1973 ones being all Alexander bodied, a mix of two 41 seat coaches, and 10 45 seat buses, the final five being 53 seat buses. The 1974 ones were 4 Duple 41 seat coaches and 14 Alexander 45 seat buses. To ease the vehicle shortage two Massey Bodied Regent Vs which originated with Baxters of Airdrie came from Scottish Omnibuses and a couple of 29 seat Bedfords arrived from Midland; there also being a loan of Bristol coaches from Western SMT and Scottish Omnibuses for use on the new Aberdeen - London service; those from Western being returned at the end of the summer service and those from Scottish Omnibuses were borrowed for the Christmas and New Year period.

Fords again dominated the 1975 deliveries but there were 6 42 seat Leyland Leopards, these being fitted with toilets and Alexander built the M type bodies, being 12 metres long, these being for the Aberdeen-London service which had until these vehicles were delivered been operated using 'borrowed' coaches from other SBG Companies. Three Leyland PD3s were also taken over from Western SMT having been on loan since June 1975, and a couple of Leyland Leopards with Alexander M type bodies were acquired from Scottish Omnibuses to strengthen the long distance express fleet, plus a single Ford on loan from Highland Omnibuses which was used on the Aberdeen-Corby service, and later returned once the two Leopards had been received from SOL.

1976 was another all Ford year for new additions, this time with all bodywork being supplied by Duple. Western SMT's provision in 1976 were six Albion Lowlanders, and six Leyland Leopards came from Central along with six Daimler Fleetlines, the first rear engined deckers in the Northern fleet.

1977 saw Duple bodies on 11 Leyland Leopards, but more unusually, 7 Ford R1114 chassis received Dominant E type bodies, on which Duple used a coach shell but fitted 53 bus seats and simplified the external trim. The balance of Fords had Alexander bodies and brought the grand total of

Fords operated up to 189. Double deckers received were all ex Midland, being 14 Fleetlines with a mixture of ECW, NCME and Alexander bodies. Five Leyland Leopards also came from Highland in exchange for five Fords..

1978 was a lean year with only 8 new Daimler Fleetline double deckers arriving with ECW bodies. More Leopards, 6 with Duple and 10 with Alexander bodies arrived in 1979 and 5 more Fords. There were 28 Leyland Leopards delivered in 1980, 19 with Alexander 53 seat bus bodies, and 5 each with Duple and Alexander coach bodies. Western SMT provided seven Daimler Fleetlines new in 1965 and 1966. There were also 5 more Fords, and the first Leyland Nationals, 8 short Mk1s, 4 short Mk2s, and 6 long Mk2s. Leyland's new Olympian double decker made its first appearance in the fleet in 1981 and there were 10 with Alexander and 21 with ECW bodies, deliveries carrying over into 1982, There were also 7 of Leyland's new Tiger chassis which replaced the Leopard, but six of these had Duple Goldliner bodies for express service use with 49 seats and toilet, the other was a 28 seat coach originally dedicated for the use of Aberdeen Football Club. The last Leopards arrived and these were 10 53 seat buses with Alexander Y type bodies; the Y type was coming to the end of its 20 year or so run, but two trial vehicles, both with this type of body were delivered in 1983 for evaluation, a Dennis Lancet and a Volvo B57. 10 more Olympians also arrived in 1983, along with 5 Leyland Tigers bodied as coaches by Duple and 7 bodied as 52 seat buses with Alexander's new P type bodies.

Four more Olympians arrived in 1984, along with 5 more Dennis Lancets 7 and Leyland Tigers with Alexander bus bodies, and 2 MCW Metroliner coaches with MCW 48 seat bodies equipped with toilets., but the most interesting arrival was a double deck Metroliner coach which had been a demonstrator. It was joined by another example bought new. The latest coach ideas were incorporated in the 5 MCW Hiliners delivered in 1985; these were high floored coaches of the style which has predominated in the coach industry since then. The two Leyland Royal Tigers delivered in 1985 were unusual in having Roe Doyen bodies with 46 seats and toilets and were delivered in London livery. There were also 7 Leyland Tigers with Alexander coach bodies for Citylink work. There were two final Tigers which passed to Strathtay on the reorganisation, and the last vehicles to be mentioned in this resume are 13 more Olympians with Alexander bodies.

The 1985 reorganisation saw a redistribution of vehicles from all three former Alexander Companies, with both Midland and Northern losing vehicles to Strathtay, Midland losing vehicles to Kelvin but gaining vehicles from Highland and some from Eastern following the acquisition of Oban, B'oness and Linlithgow. Fife stayed virtually untouched.

To today's observer, little remains of the empire which we set out to record for posterity in both this volume and the previous book. Thankfully some of the vehicles are in preservation and we can but get a feel of how things were 'once upon a time'.

Garages

FIFE: Headquarters Esplanade Kirkcaldy.

Garages: Anstruther (A), Aberhill (AL), Cowdenbeath (C), Cupar (CR), Dunfermline (D), Kelty (KY), Kirkcaldy (K), Lochgelly (LY), Newburgh (N), St. Andrews (STA).

Note: Dunfermline Market Street (D2) was closed in 1961

MIDLAND: Headquarters Brown Street, Camelon, Falkirk.

Garages: Alloa (A). Balfron (B), Bannockburn (BN), Crieff (C), Callander (CL) - later a subsidiary of Stirling from 1967, Cumbernauld (CD) - opened 1967 to replace Glenboig acquired via Carmichael takeover, , Grangemouth (G), Kilsyth (K), Kirkintilloch (KH), Larbert (L), Milngavie (M), Oban (ON) - transferred to Highland in 1970, Perth (P), Pitlochry (PY), Stepps (SS), Stirling (S).

NORTHERN: Headquarters Gairn Terrace, Hardgate, Aberdeen.

Registered Office Bus Station, Guild Street, Aberdeen

Garages: Aberdeen (A), Arbroath (AH), Blairgowrie (BL), Buckie (B), Dundee (D) (D2), Elgin (E), Forfar (FR), Fraserburgh (F) opened in October 1975, Fyvie (F), Huntly (H), Macduff (MF), Montrose (M), Peterhead (P), Rosehearty (R) - replaced by Fraserburgh in October 1975, Stonehaven (S).

Notes: There were also sub-depots at Alford, Forres, Fyvie, Methlick, Mintlaw, Strathdon and Turriff, vehicles being manned by local crews and brought into the nearest depot for maintenance when required.

The former SMT Dundee depot in Westfield Avenue (D2) closed in the 1950s.

1. *Northern inherited the lions share of the AEC Regals, 78 in all. Typical of these was NA45 seen in Montrose in Northern livery. This particular vehicle lasted until 1967, indeed Northern's half cabs were the last in regular operation in the British Isles.*

2. *Old axe, old handle! A93 was new to James Sutherland, Peterhead in November 1938 with a Duple coach body. It received the second-hand Alexander body shown here in 1953. This body was one of a number released when SMT Regals were lengthened and fitted with new Burlingham Seagull bodies in 1952/3. It lasted until 1964. It is seen on 'home' territory inside Peterhead garage.*

3. *Midland only retained 25 Regals, all of these bar one being Burlingham bodied examples new in 1946-7. Grangemouth's A66 is seen here on the Grangemouth Circular in Callander Riggs bus station Falkirk. By now the two tone blue bus livery had given way to all azure blue with ivory relief. All were gone, including the 10 AEC Regal IIIs, by 1964.*

4. *Another ex-Sutherland vehicle was A97, an AEC Regal new in 1947. Unlike sister A96 this one stayed on home territory until withdrawn in 1965. Seen in yellow livery it was delivered new from Brush of Loughborough in Sutherland's attractive red, cream and grey, losing this for Alexanders blue after just over three years.*

5. *Alexanders last Regals were new in 1951 and were 6 MkIIIs delivered in May 1951. The 35 seat coach bodies were 8' wide and all finished up in the Northern area. Arbroath's NA103 is seen here in Dundee laying over before returning to the land of 'Smokies'. All lasted in service until 1971/ 2, A99 having the distinction of being the last Alexanders half-cab single decker in service - almost!*

6. *The 'almost' in the last caption is because Northern inherited 3 AEC Regal IIIs from Burnett's Motors of Mintlaw on the takeover of January 1967. All three had come from City of Oxford Motor Services in December 1963, but only NA106 lasted until 1972, and was the only one to receive Northern bus livery as seen here. Note the modifications made to allow for one man operation which were effected by Burnetts. Thankfully this vehicle OJO727 is now lovingly restored to City of Oxford livery and resides at the Oxford bus museum.*

7. *Northern only acquired four of the Daimler CVD6 single deckers, and Stonehaven continued to use them on private hire work as well as the occasional stage service. Stonehaven's ND19 and ND20 are seen here, in Northern's version of coach livery in which the former azure blue had become yellow.*

8. *ND12 is seen here after withdrawal in 1970 and has acquired bus livery, as had sister ND10, these two vehicles being based at Elgin and used as buses. They outlasted their Midland counterparts by some 5 years.*

9. *Midland was the home for the 13 ECW bodied Daimlers, all thirteen being withdrawn en masse at the end of 1965. The first of the batch MD36 has received Midland fleet number plates, but this Larbert based vehicle still displays 'Bluebird' on the front offside screen.*

10. *Of 101 Guy Arab single deckers still in service in 1961, only 22 came to Midland and these ex Lawsons vehicles were G4-21 plus G1-2 and G31-2 . The Lawson identity was to vanish with the split, but for a moment we look back and see G1, the first of the Duple bodied Guys, in the garage yard at Kirkintilloch.*

11. *The rest of the Guys went to Fife, and here FG51, one of the Brockhouse bodied examples, is seen in Fife bus livery without depot plates but obviously operating from Newburgh depot where the vehicle finished its working life in 1968.*

12. *All the Massey bodied Guys were to be found in Fife and Aberhill's FG66 heads for East Wemyss.*

13. There were still 171 prewar Leyland Tigers on the strength in 1961 at the time of the split-up. Fife retained Fife inherited 40 including P539 seen here which was retained in coach livery to enable it to operate a tour which used the Queensferry Passage on which there was a weight restriction for commercial vehicles. All Fife's prewar single deckers, including P539, had gone by 1963, the opening of the Forth Road Bridge enabled all Fife's vehicles to reach Edinburgh.

14. Midland inherited 82 of which 16 were TS8s. The remainder were the famous TS8 specials and a number of these survived to be repainted into Midland livery. The Brown Street overhaul works at Camelon was still capable of turning out some impressive overhauls in the 1960s and here is Stirling's P655 with a fresh coat of paint - it was finally withdrawn and scrapped by the operator in 1963.

15. P674 is seen in Callander Riggs, Falkirk. This was one of the last prewar single deckers to go in 1964 finishing up with Millburn Motors. Many of these vehicles were in as good a condition as they ever were on withdrawal, and it is sad that a complete and sound example has not survived into preservation.

16. *199 of the ubiquitous Leyland Tiger PS1s were still in service in 1961 and 94 went to Midland. Larbert's PA47 displays the original style of fleetname used after the split; it was simply the original transfer with the "& Sons Ltd" cut out and replaced with "& Sons (Midland) Ltd." MPA47 lasted until 1968.*

17. Northern inherited 60 PS1s and NPA19 is seen outside Dundee garage in Northern's bus livery. This vehicle remained in service until 1970.

18. Newburgh's PA49 was one of 45 PS1s taken into the Fife fleet and is seen here in Fife red heading for Perth, one of the few places where ordinary vehicles of all three Companies could be seen together. 1969 saw the end of the road for this vehicle, which like the other two on this page display the early postwar version of the Alexander 35 seat body. Due to material shortages some of these vehicles had timber framed bodies but the end result was indistinguishable from the standard metal framed variety.

19. Fife's FPA78 is about
to leave home ground at
Dunfermline for Culross,
that historic little town
further west along the
northern shores of the
Firth of Forth.   The
conductress is busy filling
in her waybill but there
are no passengers as yet!
Withdrawn in 1967 this
vehicle finished up in
Muirs   scrapyard   in
Kirkcaldy, the graveyard
of most of Fife's fleet.

20.   Aberdeen's NPA142
shows off Northern livery
and of course the later style
of Alexander body.   Note
how the window glasses
have   been   reset   using
rubber mountings;   this
method of glazing was
commonly   used   when
refurbishing the later style
of body.

. Midland's MPA176, fresh
om overhaul and showing
e type of side window used
 the   final   batches   of
exander bodies in 1950-2 is
so interesting in that it
splays the style of trim used
 the PB class of OPS2s.
rther research would show
at this vehicle and perhaps
handful of others near the
d of the batch received this
im as they were turned out
ter a batch of replacement
dies on TS8 special chassis
r Western SMT and no doubt
ocks of beading would be
ed up.

22. New to James Sutherland PA202 with its Duple body waits to return to Stonehaven from Aberdeen. In bus livery the body also shows signs of attention at the works with rubber mounted windows and top sliders replacing the original half-drop units. New in September 1949 these fine vehicles finished up with a Lanarkshire contractor in 1969 and then went for scrap.

23. Sister vehicle NPA198 is seen at Aberdeen Station by which time it had moved to Rosehearty depot, being employed on bus work from there. Although this vehicle no longer exists, sister NPA197 is now in the Maypole Coaches fleet at Blackpool.

24. There were 14 of these Burlingham bodied Leyland Tiger PS1s new in 1950 and Northern inherited 9. Elgin's NPA204 lasted until 1971 and these units were used mainly on bus work in their twilight years; the limited destination equipment allowing liberal use of 'stickers'.

25. *The OPS2 coaches were in the main shadows of their former selves due to the donation of parts of seventeen of them to create the Midland PD3/3Cs. Northern inherited 4, and the painted radiator shows that NPB11 is one of those with axles, running units and other parts from withdrawn PS1s as were the other three.*

26. *Fife got 10 OPS2s, including PB19 which was one of the three not converted to PS1 standard, the others being PB7 and PB20 also to be found in the Fife area. It is seen with FPA158 in Dunfermline depot.*

27. *Still in coach livery but with Midland fleetnames, PB13 shows evidence of its continued use on the Glasgow-Oban service as it awaits further activity, parked in Killermont Street, Glasgow with Buchanan Street Goods Station behind. MPB13 outlasted Buchanan Street by 2 years being withdrawn in 1970. The 7'6" wide axles are easily noticed on this vehicle which had donated its original running units to create RB253.*

28. The prewar Titans still around in 1961 were mainly to be found in the Midland area, indeed there were 65 of them still on the strength. Midland later inherited another of Northern's original 16 and there were 12 in the Fife area. One of their last stamping grounds was on the busy routes out of Glasgow, indeed Milngavie still had a sizeable allocation in 1961. Here R230, complete with altered fleetname and new legal ownership lettering, reposes in Milngavie garage yard.

29. Surrounded by grey tenement buildings in Glasgow's Renfrew Street R231 rests between journeys on the 11C between Glasgow and Milngavie Cross. R231 outlasted Glasgow's trams by around six months being withdrawn in April 1963.

30. RO458 was one of the wartime Guy Arabs whose life was extended (in theory) by the fitting of new ECW bodies in 1951 and had come to Midland from the Lawsons fleet. Still allocated to Kirkintilloch but now in Midland blue one can but speculate on the conversation between the crew who appear to have abandoned their charge, no doubt to take a 'cuppa' before another run to Campsie Glen. The new bodies on these vehicles did not prolong their lives, indeed RO458 had gone by October 1965.

31. The Fife area was the stamping ground of most of the highbridge Guy Arabs and Dunfermline's FRO482 shows of the Fife red livery as it reposes at the depot. The Northern Counties body has been rebuilt with new window pans. Fife inherited 98 Arab double deckers at the split-up.

32. The vehicles operating the Kirkcaldy town services were traditionally painted in a dark red livery which was the same as that employed on Perth City and Lawsons buses. With Fife adopting Ayres Red, which was a lighter shade, as standard the buses operating the Kirkcaldy town services were fitted with boards as seen here on RO515 as it makes an extra journey to Kirkcaldy High School.

33. Fife was also the home of the 25 Cravens bodied Guy Arab IIIs new in 1948 and these lasted around another 8-9 years with the Fife Company. The Cravens bodied Guys in red showed even more resemblance to the Craven bodied RTs for London Transport. FRO590 and FRO591 await further duties and it is interesting to note the self advertising which Fife employed in the mid 1960s.

34. There were 9 Daimler CWA6 double deckers which Northern had inherited which were new to Sutherland of Peterhead and a surprise came when they were transferred to Midland in 1962 along with 4 Titan TD7s. The Titans were soon withdrawn but the Daimlers lasted a little longer and seen here at Kilsyth garage is RO684 which had a Duple lowbridge utility body and was new in June 1945.

35. Also new to Sutherlands in March 1946 was RO689, seen at Stepps between RA34 and RB116. It has a Massey Bros. of Wigan body. As with all Sutherlands double deckers platform doors were fitted.

36. Parked at the top of Killermont Street, Glasgow, MRA16 from Milngavie depot shows the early postwar Alexander body, which in detail was similar to the wartime rebuilds of TS7 single deckers.

It is said that the perpetuation of this style of body even after Alexanders had built 50 bodies for Leyland to peacetime standards was to use up stocks of parts and also there was a shortage of skilled panel beaters at the time - the wartime domes were more easily produced.

37. The bodies on RA31 upwards were of this style as seen on MRA43. The result was almost indistinguishable from the current Leyland design but there were subtle differences as Alexanders used a separate offside front mudguard on PD1s, and the horizontal panel strapping on Alexander bodies below the windows was flat, on Leyland bodies it was rounded.

38. Alexanders had no Leyland bodied PD1s of their own, those appearing in the Northern fleet had come from James Sutherland of Peterhead in 1950. NRA98 is seen in Aberdeen and had sported platform doors from new, indeed the rear of sister NRA100 can just been seen to good effect in the picture. When platform doors were fitted to double deckers a separate emergency exit had to be provided as seen here.

39. Dundee's NRB 75 displays the early version of Northern's double deck livery with lining out on the upper deck panels. It is about to depart for the seaside town of Carnoustie, famous for golf and a popular holiday destination for west of Scotland folk before package holidays took them overseas. The busy service provided by Alexander's Northern followed the route of the former Dundee and Broughty Ferry Tramways Co.

40. *Midland's MRB89 performing on a Glasgow local to Drumchapel still shows the Leyland outline but by the time this vehicle arrived Alexanders had adopted a different style of window glazing with flush window pans.*

41. *There were a dozen of these Leyland Titan PD2/12s new in 1951 with Leyland Faringdon style bodies and they all survived the split apart from RB112 which was burnt out in July 1956 and scrapped. They were mainly employed around the Glasgow area being allocated latterly to Milngavie or Stepps garages, but some had been at Grangemouth when new. Milngavie's RB113 rests between arduous duties to the Glasgow housing estates. The whole batch was withdrawn in 1970, MRB113 later becoming a driver training vehicle with the General School of Motoring along with MRB114 and MRB116.*

42. *Midland inherited 19 of the PD2s with Alexander bodies out of a total of 62 of the curvaceous style commencing at RB106. But for something which looks almost the same but not quite here is RA5 which was new in 1948 fitted with a second-hand Burlingham body. Rebodied and re-registered in 1955 this PD1 shows one obvious difference to its similar cousins in that it is only 7' 6" wide.*

43. Northern's RB161 sports one of the experimental liveries used in 1962 with a cream tween-decks band. This was a 1953 Leyland Titan PD2/12, the chassis being designed for 27' long bodywork which became legal in 1950. The PD2/12 had a wheelbase 2 inches longer than the PD2/3 - the Alexander bodies however had already pre-empted the change and were to full 27' length most of the extra space being on the platform. The scene is Denburn, with the library, St. Mark's Church and the rear of Her Majesty's Theatre in the background. Denburn Health Centre now occupies this area and it is no longer possible to gain access to Denburn from the east.

44. Seen in the final livery chosen by Northern for its 'deckers is RB140, a 1951 Leyland Titan PD2/3. It is seen in the new bus station adjacent to Aberdeen Joint Railway Station opened in 1963. The advertisement is noteworthy, as at one time SMT sales and service were part of the same SMT group as Alexanders but like Alexander's coachbuilding activities, became independent on the nationalisation of the SMT group's passenger transport interests in 1948.

45. Fife's Ayres red suited the curvaceous lines of the 1950 Alexander body well, and Dunfermline's FRB 142 was one of 16 of the type taken into Fife stock. Even in the mid 1960s it was necessary to maintain a proportion of the fleet for schools, works, and extra duties with the result that a number of vehicles spent part of the day idle.

46. *Alexanders took no new Leyland double deckers between 1953 and 1958, and the first of the 30 footers arrived in that year starting with RB168.   Northern inherited 8 of the first batch and RB196 is seen here in Northern livery on the busy suburban route to Dyce, home then of Lawsons sausages and today of Aberdeen airport.   The statue of William Wallace looks on, Wallace Statue being the City centre timing point on this cross City service from Culter, the frequency of which was enhanced by extra vehicles during the summer.*

47. *This experimental livery was tried on Midland's PD3s; at least it brightens up the dismal harled walls in central Glasgow as Milngavie's MRB224, one of the 1960 batch waits to go and take up its turn in Killermont Street before taking a load of shoppers out to the suburbs.   All three Companies adopted the script style of fleetname from 1962.*

48. *Midland's Titans were later enhanced with the addition of three ivory bands as seen here on Milngavie's MRB233 one of the 1960 deliveries. The later style of fleetname is evident here which was applied after 1968.   This vehicle lasted until 1975, being used latterly on extra and schools duties as seen here.*

49. Stepps' MRB247 awaits another excursion to Gartcosh at Dundas Street bus station Glasgow. One of the 'new' PD3/Cs created from the running units out of 17 of the OPS2s, these vehicles brought the exposed radiator back; of course these came off the OPS2s as did axles and engines, which were fitted into new PD3 chassis frames.

50. Sporting the experimental livery referred to previously Larbert's MRB259 is in perpetual orbit on the Falkirk Circular service, just outside Callander Riggs bus station. This route followed the tracks of the Falkirk and District Trams which were abandoned in 1936.

. Northern's own first PD3s had in fact en ordered before the split and were livered in late 1961 in blue. RB280-6 lasted til the late 1970s and spent most of their es on the busy suburban routes out of erdeen, being finally ousted when the OMO slaught gathered apace. RB286 was the st PD3 delivered new to any of the exander Companies. RB283 is seen when most new passing along Rosemount aduct with Education, Resurrection and mnation in the background, a local scription of the Library, St. Mark's Church d Her Majesty's Theatre; all of which would ve provided patronage for the buses at one ne.

52. The penultimate vehicle of the batch NRB285 in Northern livery takes a well earned rest at the back of the bus station after working on the 2 service from Culter to Dyce; it will have shortworked to the Wallace Statue before 'coming off'.

53. *Increased traffic needs due to the 'oil boom' of the early 1970s caused the transfer of 18 Leyland PD2/20s from Western SMT. NRB169 was new in 1955 and had a Northern Counties 55 seat lowbridge body. Allocated to Rosehearty, this vehicle's arrival also allowed the withdrawal of some of the ex Simpson's acquisitions.*

54. *The last seven dated from 1956 and had Alexander bodies seating 59. NRB180 was also allocated to Rosehearty and can be seen on home ground in Fraserburgh in company with one of the ex Simpson deckers of which more anon.*

55. *Midland was the home for all 20 AEC Regent IIIs, and Grangemouth's MRC17 lays over at Camelon before returning to Grangemouth through Falkirk. New in 1951 these fine vehicles were all withdrawn between 1968 and 1970. A ride 'across town' brought London sound effects to the North with the pre-selector gearbox in action.*

56. By virtue of its BTC ownership, Alexanders were able to avail themselves of Bristol and ECW products. The first Lodekka arrived in the Fife area in 1956 and Dunfermline's FRD2, looking more at home (in Tilling circles) in Ayres red than Azure blue heads east for North Queensferry, where until the Forth Road Bridge opened in 1964, this route connected with the ferries.

57. Perth's MRD85 came new to the Fair City in red livery in 1959, but by the time this shot in Kinnoull Street was taken it had acquired Midland blue livery (compare with view of sister MRD84 in Vol. 1). Hunter Crescent was a pre Second war slum clearance scheme off the Crieff Road and the route operated North East/ South East to Darnhall Drive.

58. Larbert's MRD153 was one of the first deliveries after the split in June 1961 and was one of the last batch of LD6G Lodekkas. Like most BTC operators, Alexanders used these low height vehicles on any route which required double deckers, although the bridge over the A9 in the background was one of those in the Falkirk area which required the use of lowbridge vehicles.

59. *Midland's first FLF6G Lodkekkas were delivered in May 1962 and the whole batch of twelve were allocated to Perth to replace most of the remaining ex London Guys. MRD169 sits in Mill Street outside the Sandeman Library, its usual employment at the time being on the 31D service from there to Letham (Strathtay Road) via the Crieff Road, an additional service introduced in 1965. More on these splendid vehicles in our forthcoming title "Perthshire Buses Remembered"*

60. *The second dozen were delivered in 1963 and were more widely scattered with two going to Larbert Including MRD1. shown here, three to Stirling, three to Bannockburn, and four to Kirkintilloch. MRD184 features the white windo rubbers introduced with this batch and is seen on Callander Riggs, Falkirk, on route 93 which passed the Brown Stre headquarters of Midland.*

61. *The 1964 batch numbered 10, of which Stirling's MRD191 and Bannockburn's MRD177 are seen at Bridge of Allan, their likely employment being on school extras. These were Midland's last 70 seat Lodekkas supplied new.*

62. *The saga of the Bristol VRs will be told when we reach that marque in the sequence of illustrations but their despatch south resulted in the arrival of 15 1966 vintage FLF6Gs from Eastern National. MRD204, complete with Cave Brown Cave heating system is seen at Larbert Road.*

63. *MRD207 shows that fleet number plates were not cast for these second-hand acquisitions as it heads south through Stirling towards Bannockburn. They had the distinction of being the last half cab buses operated by Midland and ran until 1979/80.*

64. *Alexander's former Northern area had never operated Lodekkas nor had the Northern Company until after the split-up until five FLFs were acquired in 1979 from Midland. These were out of the ex Eastern National batch and gave around four years service with Northern. Here NRD3 is seen at Seagate Dundee. Note the mixture of sliding and hopper ventilators unique to these vehicles, in an SBG fleet of course.*

65. The FLF6Gs when ordered from Bristol and ECW before the split accounted for 25 units, the remaining 13 of the order going to Fife, where they received Fife registration marks. Here FRD163 sits at the Shorehead, Leven, but as to what roster it is performing is anybody's guess as the blinds do not fit anything operated from that location.

66.. Fife opted for the short FS6G model when it ordered its own Lodekkas for 1963 delivery and FRD183 was one of ten delivered, being sent to Aberhill depot when new. It is seen in Leven on the 308 Kirkcaldy service.

67. Another fourteen FS6Gs arrived in 1964; note the platform doors which Fife specified on these vehicles ostensibly for operation over the Forth Road Bridge. FRD198 is seen in Dunfermline having just arrived from Saline.

68. *Fife's last eighteen Lodekkas and the last supplied to any SBG member were FRD200-17. They were of the longer variety at 31 feet, seating 76. They were finally extinct in 1981. With the bridge open, they were often to be seen in Edinburgh as is FRD206 here.*

69. *More Lodekkas arrived in Fife with the acquisition of 12 units from Central SMT in 1969. These were all 1955 examples and were operated for less than three years. At least FRD107 (note the reversion to unused numbers prior to FRD153 for this batch) has received full Fife livery when employed on Kirkcaldy town service 1 in 1970.*

70. *Three cast offs are shown here. FRE24 came from Central SMT in 1965, FRB102 was one of two Highbridge Leyland PD2s bought by Alexanders in 1950 'off the peg' from Leyland stock; these being the only new highbridge vehicles in the fleet until the Ailsas came, and finally FRD112, still in Central SMT livery from whence it came in 1965.*

71. The Scottish Bus group developed a love/hate relationship with certain types of vehicle in the 1960s and 1970s, and the Albion Lowlander was certainly one of them. The group wanted an economical lowheight double decker and Leyland Motors entrusted the work to Albions, hence the badging. What you got was a Titan PD3 front end married to a low frame, and appearances were not aided by the Alexander bodywork. Anyway Midland got 44 in 1963 in batches of 26 and 18. Here, in original livery, is MRE3 toddling out of Falkirk on the main A9 road towards Laurieston on the 99 service to Langlees and Westquarter.

72. Larbert's MRE6 displays the fleetname style used by Midland from 1965 until 1968 as it performs on Falkirk local service 93.. The local filmgoers can pay their 1/9d to see the Broken Lance and see Spencer Tracy perform at the ABC cinema. The raised seats on the front of the upper deck can be clearly seen and these obstructed the view ahead for all other top deck travellers.

73. Following complaints regarding the front end layout of MRE1-26 the second batch received modified bodies with a deeper nearside canopy and the nearside front upper deck seats at the same level as the rest of the upper deck. Larbert's MRE40 is seen here - note the different destination indicators fitted to this batch.

74. Northern got only 2 Lowlanders in 1963 and when new they were the first forward entrance double deckers in that fleet. They also sported offside illuminated advertisement panels when new which were later removed. No further new double deck vehicles went to Northern until 1978, and the two Lowlanders were also subjected to livery experimentation when new. NRE2 sits in the sun in Aberdeen in front of Union Terrace Gardens whilst operating the busy cross city service 2 along the Great Western Road. The city centre timing point for this route was 21 Union Terrace.

75. Fife got its only new Lowlanders, 7 of them, in 1963. Cowdenbeath's FRE7 waits at Dunfermline's Carnegie Street stance before returning to Ballingry on the busy 314 service deep in Fife coalfield territory through Cowdenbeath, Crossgates and Lochgelly.

76. The rest of Fife's Lowlanders were second-hand from Central SMT and Western SMT in 1965-7. 17 came from Central in 1965, The first of which, FRE8, still in Central livery, is seen in Dunfermline. Note how the Northern Counties body fits the design much better.

77. FRE21 came from Central and was one of only two with Alexander bodies. In a setting of harled council houses so typical of Scotland this vehicle now repainted in Fife red, heads back to Dunfermline from Ballingry.

78. A further 9 Lowlanders came from Western in 1966 and a final five from the same source in 1967. Seen in Dunfermline heading for Townhill on the cross town service from Rumblingwell, FRE27 is still in Western livery.

79. FRE34 however is now turned out in Fife livery when photographed in Glenrothes. The development of this new town in the 1960s brought additional business to the buses.

80. *Troubles behind! Alexanders succumbed to their first rear engined double deckers in 1967, Midland receiving 45 in 1967. They were Daimler Fleetline CRG6LX models with Alexander 75 seat lowheight bodies. MRF16, based at Stepps, heads into Glasgow down Parliamentary Road with Skelly's Ford garage in the background, selling the very cars that would deprive Alexanders of much of its business in the future.*

81. *The second part of the 1967 delivery featured this new style of livery with cream window surrounds. MRF 25 is seen sitting at Milngavie Garage when almost new. The livery did not last and standard livery as seen on MRF16 above was soon substituted.*

82. *A further 25 Fleetlines arrived in 1968, and Grangemouth's MRF63 is seen in Callander Riggs Falkirk about to head home on the 83A. One man operation was gaining ground when this photograph was taken and most Fleetlines received illuminated signs and Setright stands for this purpose. This particular vehicle has received a later front panel following accident damage.*

83. The 1970 deliveries to Midland included MRF82 seen here in Glasgow when operating from Milngavie garage. There were 27 in all, of which 15 had Alexander bodies, and it was observed in the Scottish Transport Group annual report for that year that operating costs of such vehicles were considerably higher than those of orthodox front engined double deckers.

84. The remaining 12 Fleetlines delivered in 1970 had ECW bodies and MRF94 shows an attempt at getting fleet and registration numbers in accord. Seen later in life with Midland Scottish fleetnames introduced in 1978 this Milngavie based bus had yet to receive PAYE signs.

85. MRF92 is seen at Larbert on the Circular. At the time that the photograph was taken a faded wooden notice on the bridge advised tram passengers not to touch the overhead wire. Nine similar vehicles dating from 1971 came to Midland from Central SMT in 1975.

86.   Only four Fleetlines arrived for Midland in 1971 and these had the new alloy A type Alexander bodies which featured a more rounded roof profile. MRF99 is seen on the Falkirk circular. Another four virtually identical vehicles arrived in 1973.

87.   No new double deckers were bought in 1974 and 1975, the eleven 1976 purchases being similar to those bought in 1973. MRF127 is seen at Larbert Road with later Midland Scottish fleetnames.

88.   Midland returned to ECW for its 1979 bodies on Fleetline chassis and these featured wraparound windscreens. MRF142 is seen at the new Buchanan Bus Station on the busy Glasgow suburban route to Campsie Glen.

89.   Midland's last Fleetlines came in 1980 and reverted to Alexander bodywork. MRF164 is seen taking part in trials which were conducted using 4 different types of double decker in 1981 on the Glasgow-Drumchapel route 105.

90.   We now return to cover Fife's Fleetlines which only numbered 72 in total and were all delivered between 1968 and 1971.   One of the first batch, FRF4 performs on Kirkcaldy town service 12A.

91.   ECW bodied FRF37 is returning to Kirkcaldy from Leslie.   This was one of six of this type new in 1971.

92. *The 1971 deliveries to Fife were a mix of ECW, Alexander and Northern Counties bodies. One of the 19 Alexander bodied examples, FRF49, awaits further duties in a changing Kirkcaldy.*

93. *There were only five with Northern Counties bodies, all going to Midland in 1975. Here FRF72 is seen in Leven as it heads for Kennoway on a damp day.*

94. *Fife's last new Fleetline was FRF73 which was new in 1973 and was exhibited at the Scottish Motor Show that year. It is seen at Esplanade works Kirkcaldy in company with an Ailsa - note the difference in height!.*

95. *A surprise purchase in 1983 were three Fleetlines from Tayside Regional Transport. The first, FRF74 is seen in Dundee, its former home, heading for St. Andrews.*

96. *Northern inherited 20 Fleetlines from other members of the Scottish Bus Group in 1977. NRF18 came from Midland and is seen in Aberdeen heading west along Union Street for Culter.*

97. *NRF10 also came from Midland and is seen, again in Union Street, turning into Union Terrace operating the same service as NRF18 (above) but in the opposite direction. For an illustration of Northern's only new Fleetlines, see page 111, plate C23.*

98. *Goosecroft Bus Station Stirling is the location for this shot of MRT9 loading to return to Falkirk on the 75A. There were 15 of these Bristol VRTs with Gardner engines but they only lasted barely 18 months with Midland before being exchanged for Lodekkas.*

99. *A rear view of a Bristol VRT, this time of MRT8 heading north through the centre of Stirling with the new Thistle centre under construction in the background. The construction of Stirling's new shopping centre cut off the direct route to Goosecroft Road from Murray Place which many of the routes once used to gain access to the bus station.*

100. *Seen in its new home, still in Midland blue but with Eastern National fleetnames, former MRT4 is trusted with the Limited Stop service 400 when seen in Victoria Coach Station London in 1972.*

101. *Dissatisfied with rear engined double deckers, all the Alexander companies looked elsewhere for a solution to their problems, and this resulted in the development of the Volvo-Ailsa B55 double decker. This demonstrator was built in 1973 for the Scottish bus group and had Alexander 79 seat bodywork. The use of a turbocharged engine mounted at the front of the chassis left room for the driver and entrance. It finished off as a demonstrator in the Far East. The vehicle is seen here on school contract work.*

102. *Midland's first production Ailsas went to Perth initially, the last place where highbridge double deckers had been operated in 1963, these being wartime Guy Arabs. There were 14 of them and MRA7 is seen here in Mill Street Perth with the North Church and Sandeman Library in the background. The Mill Street - Letham route is still one of Perth's busiest.*

103. *Fife took the Ailsa in greater numbers, receiving 40 in 1975. FRA3 is seen here turning into Carnegie Place Dunfermline on local route 1 to Beatty Place. OMO operation is evident here and this spread gradually over the whole of the former Alexanders empire.*

104. FRA9-15 were delivered after the annual change of suffix letter on 1st August and so had P registrations. A contrast in liveries is seen here with FRA12 in the traditional red and FRA20 with cream tween-decks panels to carry an advertisement for Laidlaws the main Ford dealers.

105. There were six more Ailsas delivered in 1977 and FRA46, the last, is seen leaving the new Kirkcaldy Bus Station on a local service. By the time this photograph was taken, the route numbers listed in Vol. 1. of "Alexanders Buses Remembered" had been replaced by new series for various localities.

106. The 20 Ailsas delivered in 1979 were MkII models, easily spotted because of the higher driving position and the resulting higher windscreen. They were delivered new with white tween decks panels but soon lost these. FRA65 went on loan to Midland as TB3 in 1981 and ran alongside three other vehicles, A Central Dennis Dominator, a Midland Fleetline and the prototype Olympian.

107. FRA75 was one of two Volvo Citybus chassis bodied by Alexander with RVC type coach bodies seating 70. They were delivered in Citylink colours and it is seen on the Express Glenrothes-Glasgow service in Buchanan bus station Glasgow. Newburgh Garage was responsible for this vehicle at the time.

108. Fife's 10 Ailsas with bus bodywork delivered in 1985 along with 8 delivered in 1984 had the new R type bodywork of which the coach above was a derivative. It is seen here 'on show' with other double deckers from the group in Buchanan bus station Glasgow.

109. Midland, with its inheritance of low bridges, took on board the MCW Metrobus and this is one of three with Alexander AD type bodies delivered in 1979. It is seen in Glasgow.

110. By the time the next batch of ten arrived in 1981 Alexander had replaced the A type body with the R type and MRM11 is seen leaving Glasgow for Drumchapel.

111. More arrived between 1982 and 1985 bringing the total operated by Midland up to 104, but Kelvin and Strathtay took some each on the next reorganisation leaving Midland with only 26. Their main stamping ground was on the busy suburban services from Glasgow and MRM44 went to Kelvin Scottish.

112. MRO1 was one of Leyland's prototype Olympians and was bodied by ECW. After being shown at the 1980 Motor Show in Midland livery it went on trial with the other vehicles already mentioned in early 1981. It is seen leaving Buchanan bus station during those trials.

113. MRO1 became NLO1 in mid 1981 and paved the way for more of these vehicles to join the Northern fleet. It is seen in Aberdeen. Note the retention of the non standard livery with the blue translated into yellow.

114. A further 21 Olympians were delivered in 1982 with ECW bodies. NLO23 is one of those which remained with Northern after the 1985 reorganisation and is seen here in Fraserburgh.

115. The rest of the 1982 Olympians had Alexander bodies and NLO10 is seen heading east through Broughty Ferry before it was to be transferred to the Strathtay fleet in 1985.

116.   The era of overall advertising reached the north-east in 1982 with NLO6 being turned out in this scheme advertising McEwans Export.   It is seen in Aberdeen suitably surrounded by licensed premises.

117.   Deliveries of Olympians continued through 1983-4 and as a result of the co-operation between Grampian Regional Transport and Northern 20 were painted in Grampian Scottish livery. NLO43 is seen far from home however when on display at Glasgow's Buchanan Bus Station.

118.   The Leyland Atlantean was never purchased new by any of the Scottish Bus Group, but 10 came to Fife from Grampian Regional Transport in 1984. They were new in 1973 and their highbridge layout of the Alexander AL bodies proved no problem in the Fife area.   FRN2 is seen in Dunfermline with the marketing slogans which the group began to apply in 1985. This vehicle, in common with the others and three similar Fleetlines had lost its centre exit when this photograph was taken.

119. Northern inherited over half the AEC Reliances and Monocoaches, 94 to be precise. Seen on the Arbroath town service is NAC15, a 1954 Reliance with Park Royal 45 seat bodywork. This vehicle is unusual in being painted in coach livery, but there were a number of anomalies, as always, with Alexanders paint schemes.

120. Midland took the other 104 Reliances and Monocoaches and this scene at Dundas Street Bus Station shows Stepps' MAC25, a Monocoach with Park Royal body, on the local service to Annathill via Muirhead and Glenboig. The second style of Midland fleetname is seen here, whilst ex Lawsons MRD53 shows the first style.

121. NAC67 was one of those Monocoaches bodied by Alexander and it is seen here in Aberdeen in Northern bus livery. It ran until 1975.

122. *Coach livery this time indicates that NAC126, seen in Aberdeen having just arrived from Fraserburgh, is a 41 seater with dual purpose status. It continued to ply the North east's roads until 1977 and was a Rosehearty based vehicle moving to Fraserburgh for the last year or so of its life.*

123. *MAC173 was new in 1960 and operated in the Lawson fleet from June 1960 until May 1961, hence the 37 seats instead of 41 for extended tour work. It is seen here at Kings Cross in London whilst on such duties - a keen eye will spot the LLC for Lawsons Land Cruises on the antimacassars.*

124. *NAC186 is seen not far from another tourist area but is on normal stage carriage work at Ballater Station before setting off for Braemar, passing Balmoral Castle on the way. A 41 seater, this vehicle lasted until 1977. As the date of the photograph is uncertain, we can but speculate as to whether trains have ceased to connect with the bus - the last ones ran from Aberdeen to Ballater on 28th February 1966.*

125 . Midland took delivery of 5 Reliances in 1963, the first with Alexander Y type bodies. Kilsyth's MAC213 is seen on private hire work complete with antimacassars.

126. The immediate Alexander body design before the arrival of the Y type was one derived from vehicles being supplied to the BET group at the time to which was grafted a standard front end which was also favoured by North Western Road Car. Seen in the depot yard at Kirkcaldy is FAC8, new in 1962 as one of Fife's first batch of Reliances. There were two styles of body, the dual purpose one is seen here with roof mounted destination boxes and a power operated folding door.

127. Seen in Inverness loading before a return south is FPA9, one of those with coach trim and one piece doors, and the destination equipment below the windscreen.

128. *Fife's next Reliances had Y type bodies and were 41 seat coaches. There were fourteen of them and the last of the batch is seen here on private hire work.*

129. *For 1964 Fife took another 19 AECs, but this time there were the first 36 footers in the shape of six 49 seat coaches as exemplified here by FAC28, seen at Kirkcaldy about to leave for Edinburgh via the Forth Road Bridge.*

130. *There were also 5 53 seat buses, which featured short window bays and FAC34, the first of these, is seen leaving Leonard Street Bus Station, Perth, for Kirkcaldy. Prior to the opening of this facility buses left from the Station Square or Tay Street.*

131. *Finally, 1964 saw the arrival of 7 more 41 seat coaches, and Kirkcaldy FAC42 is seen heading out of Dunfermline for Saline. The lack of this destination on the Kirkcaldy blinds may have something to do with the use of a sticker in the windscreen.*

132. *Fife's final Reliances were more 49 seaters which arrived in 1966. Seen escaping from the 'Kingdom' is FAC53. The 355 route from Leven to Newport via the Fife coast was extended into Dundee following the opening of the Tay Road Bridge. Passengers making the Tay crossing will have been issued with special Insert Setright tickets endorsed 'Fare Includes Bridge Toll'.*

133. *Alexander's Northern area before 1961 was very much AEC territory and the arrival of Reliances continued with 18 arriving in 1962. There were 8 41 seat coaches like NAC204 seen here in Arbroath.*

134. The remainder were 45 seat buses and NAC 212 awaits its next duty in Aberdeen. The style of bus seat fitted to Alexanders single deckers had changed little from the TS8s of 1938 as can be seen by peering into this vehicle and comparing it with the interior shots in Vol. 1.

135. The 1963 deliveries were all 41 seat coaches with Y type bodies and there were 22 of them. Stonehaven's NAC236 is seen in Aberdeen having arrived from Dundee. The first 12 however had manual doors and more comfortable seats for dedicated coach work.

136. 1964 saw another 18 arrive again with 41 seat bodies and this shot on 24th October 1965 at Ballater Station would see a connection with the Aberdeen train, which in those latter days was a two car battery electric unit converted from a Derby lightweight DMU. The train took and hour and 25 minutes from Aberdeen whilst the bus took 2 hours and 5 minutes. These were Northern's last new Reliances and NAC249 is shown here.

137. Northern received its first 36' Reliances second-hand from Scottish Omnibuses in 1969 - there were six of them new in 1966. All had 49 seat dual purpose bodies. NAC262 is seen in Aberdeen - this vehicle was being used on the service to Dyce Airport when photographed.

138. Fife was the home of all 20 Bristol LS buses new in 1955. Lochgelly's FE7 shows off its new red livery which of course made these vehicles look very much like their English counterparts of which there were hundreds in the ex Tilling fleets. The destination display was unique to the Alexanders ones however. They all survived until 1973-5.

139. It wasn't surprising when Fife went back to Bristol and ECW for 12 Bristol RELL6Gs with 53 seat bus bodies which arrived in 1968. Kelty's FE22 is obviously looking after the needs of those requiring travel to the new town of Glenrothes. Dissatisfaction with the new generation of rear engined double deckers meant that after 1973 maximum capacity single deckers were preferred until the arrival of the Ailsas and these Gardner powered vehicles lasted until 1983.

140. Midland took batches of Bristol LH chassis from 1970 until 1972 . The 1970 deliveries had 38 seat or 41 seat coach bodies by Alexander, the front mounted radiator requiring a deviation from the normal Y type front panel. More arrived in 1971, the first of which MLH20 is seen here, and the total operated reached 41 by September 1972, the last three being seated as 45 seat buses. All had Perkins engines and the choice of this chassis may have been as an alternative to the Albion Viking, but there was the business of the SBG's quota of Bristol purchases, and saloons may have been taken instead of more VRs, ECW of course bodying Fleetlines instead. The scene is Stirling and at that time MLH20 was a Bannockburn vehicle.

141. We go back in time to cover the period when the Albion Aberdonian found favour with Alexanders, indeed two arrived in 1957 and a further 20 in 1958. Midland only kept one at the split, and Fife inherited 5 including FNL12 seen here. They were 41 seaters.

142. Northern operated 17 Aberdonians and NNL19 is seen here heading out of Aberdeen for the trip along Deeside to Braemar. There seems to be a light load on this trip but the Conductress is busy collecting fares already - there may be time to do a bit of knitting later on - a pastime which was not unknown amongst female platform staff!

143. Single deck Albions reappeared in the fleet in 1965 following the placing of substantial orders for the new rear engined Albion Viking VK43L chassis. All were fitted with Alexander Y type bodies and the first MNV1 was seated for 38. The normal seating arrangements were for 40. MNV2 is seen at Larbert Road later in its career after bus livery had been applied and conversion to OMO undertaken..

The last Viking was delivered to Midland in 1969 making 75 in all.

144. Northern took Albion Vikings until 1970. They received 88 examples from 1965 and in addition 6 came from Scottish Omnibuses in 1972. Here NNV60, one of the 1968 batch, is seen in 'Thrums' after arriving from Dundee - would some of the alighting passengers have been 'touristes' looking for the birthplace of J. M. Barrie, author of' Peter Pan'?

145. Kirkcaldy is the setting for our Fife example of the Viking, in this case FNV36 new in 1969 and seen here prepared for coach duties with antimacassars on the headrests. Fife only took 48 Vikings changing over to Bristols for the next year's single deck deliveries.

146. *Leylands always pre-dominated in the Alexander fleet before 1961, and we see one of the 1953 deliveries of Leyland Royal Tigers, with Alexander 'Coronation' bodies, in Aberdeen in Northern livery. The glazed quarterlights were a later addition to these heavy-weights of which Northern inherited 16.*

147. *Midland operated 57 of the Royd Tigers, including MPC24. Body renovation saw most examples lose the distinctive visor over the windscreens. These vehicles operated in many livery variations and this scheme was adopted in 1962. The PCs later reverted to the original livery. Although they could find use on schools and stage work to a limited extent, right until withdrawal their use on tours was commonplace.*

148. *One of the solutions to the centre entrance layout of the Royal Tigers was to convert them to front entrance. Fife converted five and Northern three, and FPC52 is seen in such a state in the garage yard at Dunfermline. The Royal Tigers in all three fleets had gone by 1972.*

149. Not all of the Royal Tigers had Alexander 'Coronation' bodies, indeed there were 10 with Leyland bodies. Northern operated NPC33 and four others of this type. The Leyland bodies had an external cab door. The location is Fraserburgh.

150. After the heavyweight Royal Tigers came the Leyland Tiger Cub, a medium weight chassis which found favour with Alexanders. The first examples arrived, with a new style of coach body, in 1954, and PD24 was one of those new to the associated Lawsons fleet for extended tour work. They continued in this role after Lawsons was absorbed and became part of Midland and this view at Kings Cross in London shows MPD24 on such duties.

151. Northern ran 10 of the original Tiger Cubs, indeed they were the sum total of this type operated, and NPD9 is seen parked up in Aberdeen. On withdrawal in 1973 this vehicle finished up in the ownership of the Dagenham Swimming Club!

152. *Fife didn't inherit any of the coach bodied Tiger Cubs. At first glance this vehicle looks like one of them but in fact it was one of 20 Guy Arab LUFs delivered in 1955 and 1957, all of which were new to the Fife area and there they stayed until the last one was withdrawn in 1972. Here FGA11 has been demoted to bus work and is operating the 378 service from Kirkcaldy to West Wemyss*

153. *A return to Leylands sees the 1955 design of Alexander bus body as applied to the Tiger Cub. MPD53, new in that year, is seen coming off Murray Place in Stirling to head for the bus station at Goosecroft to take up duty. Note the revised frontal treatment applied by Midland to some of these vehicles in later life.*

154. *Fife inherited 57 Tiger Cubs following the split, and FPD59 is seen at Kirkcaldy depot. This particular vehicle met a fateful end, being scrapped in September 1970 after accident damage. Others of the type survived until 1974.*

155. The 1958 Tiger Cubs featured a new style of Alexander body which was derived from the previous coach version but with a straight waistline. There were variations as we shall soon see however. One of the first batch MPD130, still in coach livery heads to take up duty from Stirling Garage in Forth Street, passing Thos. Muir Son & Paton's Thames Trader coal lorry parked on the pavement outside their coal office. The Stirling Dunfermline route was worked jointly by Midland and Fife.

156. The same location finds Fife's FPD164 also heading for the bus station at Goosecroft having started its journey at Leven. The turrets of Stirling's North Church can just be seen in the background. This vehicle was based at Aberhill at the time and was new in 1959. It gave good service lasting until 1975. Fife repainted most of these vehicles from blue to red in bus livery.

157. Scottish Omnibuses were not an operator of Tiger Cubs, being a predominently AEC fleet, and when Baxters were taken over in December 1962 they inherited this example, new in 1958. But note the curved waistrail applied to the later body style. This vehicle was passed to Midland in December 1962 in exchange for 1958 Reliance MAC145.

158. Midland inherited two other Tiger Cubs by way of SOL. Both were new in April 1954 as demonstrators but were acquired by Lowland Motorways later in 1954, passing to Scottish Omnibuses in January 1958 when Lowland was acquired. MPD203 is seen, when operating from Stirling, on the service which connected with the steamer 'Sir Walter Scott' at Trossachs Pier, despite the Private display on the indicator.

159. MPD204 is seen in Dock Street Dundee operating on the Limited Stop service to Edinburgh which before opening of the Forth Road Bridge operated via Perth, Stirling and Falkirk. The stickers in the window reveal this duty but the Glasgow setting on the destination blind confuses! A 4pm arrival at Stirling would, however, enable Glasgow bound passengers to go forward on another service, there being a variety of ways to get there from Stirling. Both these two vehicles lasted until 1970.

160. MPD224 managed to get its registration number out of sequence as was its chassis number. The chassis was new in 1962 and actually came before the Tiger Cubs with BET style bodies. However this vehicle did not enter service until 1963. It had a coach seated body with single piece door. The location for the photograph is Gloucester Green, Oxford whilst the vehicle was en route from Bournemouth back to Glasgow.

161. The 1961 Tiger Cubs had unique bodies with styling somewhat reminiscent of the Ford Classic and Anglia cars. There were 19 of them all but one with 38 seat bodies. MPD 207 is parked up in Glasgow awaiting tour duties - note the AMS insignia on the antimacassars! There were no more of these stylish bodies due to the moulds for the GRP front and rear panels being destroyed in a fire at Alexanders Glasgow Road, Falkirk, coachworks.

162. The 1962 Tiger Cubs had bodies derived from those being produced for BET group companies in England and were also unique to one year's deliveries. Midland received 19 in all and there were three varieties. All had seating for 41; MPD226 was one of those with coach seats and single leaf door. MPD226 was allocated to Stepps garage. It was usual for new coaches to start their life there and be passed on later to other depots.

163. There were also some with roof mounted destination boxes and jack knife doors as exemplified by MPD238 seen here on a football hire in Kilmarnock. These vehicles retained their original livery style till withdrawn.

164. The first Y types appeared 'en force' in 1963 and just compare the ambience of MPD262 on tour and laying over at London's King's Cross coach station before taking the patrons on to Bournemouth with the Eastern National MW parked alongside. What innovation with panoramic windows, wraparound front windscreen and rear windows, and inside a forced air ventilation system one would expect to find on an airliner! Alexanders got it right 'first time' and the 20 year run of this body style can truly make this body a classic of all time. Its fame spread far beyond the Scottish Bus Group.

165. With 36' single deckers now legal, Leyland launched its Leopard chassis in 1961, but it was to be three years on when Alexanders took delivery of their first 36 footers. The first 15 delivered to Midland were 49 seater coaches and Bannockburn's MPE14 heads east along the A9 having left Callander Riggs bus station a few minutes previously on a journey which will end at Edinburgh's St. Andrews Square bus station.

166. The second 15 Leopards delivered to Midland were 53 seat buses featuring short window bays and their appearance when new in coach livery may have confused some. However we only have to look back and see how many single deckers from the late 1930s were also turned out as 'Bluebirds' when new!

MPE23 is seen in a familiar location heading for Stirling bus station.

167. Deliveries of Leopards continued with Midland operating 82 examples by 1965. No new examples were added until 1969 when 8 more arrived. MPE94 is seen here at Perth bus station whilst operating the direct service to Crieff via Methven. This Bannockburn vehicle must have been on loan to Crieff at the time.

168. Midland continued to take Leopards in small numbers of both 49 seat coach and 53 seat bus varieties. Dissatisfaction with rear engined double deckers saw 27 high capacity single deckers arrive in 1972. These, however, were delivered new in bus livery. MPE142 is seen in Stirling on the Glasgow -Dunfermline route.

169. Seen at Glasgow's Buchanan bus station MPE157 was one of the 1973 batch of which only 7 were coach style, four being 44 seaters for extended tours and the remainder 49 seaters. This view shows the latter day livery with blue skirt and corporate fleetnames.

170. All 53 seat buses delivered between 1971 and 1975 featured the Y type body in its short window form, but the 13 53 seat buses delivered in 1977 had panoramic windows. There was a reason for this as these vehicles were actually part of a Western SMT order diverted to Midland; Western always specifying thus type of body even for buses. MPE244 rests at Bannockburn. OMO is here and the adjustable stand with Setright Speed can be seen through the windscreen. Bus livery is applied - of course!

171. Midland had a tradition of Duple bodies for coaches, although these were normally associated with Bedford chassis. In 1977 there were 8 Leyland Leopards with 49 seat Duple Dominant bodies. Classed as coaches, hence the Midland-Bluebird fleetnames, the roof mounted destination indicators meant that they could also find work on stage carriage services.

172. Parked at Buchanan bus station, Glasgow, MPE260 was also one of the 1977 deliveries. Although equipped for OMO there are no illuminated signs - by this time driver only operation was in danger of becoming the norm rather than the exception.

173. The 1978 Leopard deliveries included 10 coaches with the new Alexander T type body. MPE273 is seen from the rear as it arrives in Glasgow. The T type body never enjoyed the popularity of the Y type.

174. Nevertheless, Leopards with T type bodies continued to arrive and it was this body which graced the first Tigers in 1983. The Tiger replaced the Leopard, and Midland continued to take Leopards until 1982. One of the 1980 deliveries is seen here.

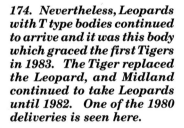

175. The last Leopards were three 53 seat buses delivered in 1982 along with a further 3 examples seated for 49. One of the 49 seaters, MPE425 which had the distinction of being Midland's last new Leopard is seen in Glasgow having come in from Stirling via Balfron, its home base.

176. The Alexander T type body was 'cleaned up' in 1983 and the result was the TE. Midland took 5 with 46 seats on Leyland Tiger chassis. About to finish its journey at Glasgow's Buchanan bus station is MPT111.

177. The other 5 Tigers delivered in 1983 had the Alexander TC type body and MPT117 is seen in Glasgow in Scottish Citylink livery.

178. Also in Citylink livery is MPT128, one of 6 delivered in 1984-5 with Duple Laser bodywork. These had 46 reclining seats and toilet for express services. This tiger is seen in Northern territory at Aberdeen.

179. Fife's reliance on Reliances meant that there were no Leopards taken until 1970 when 13 like FPE5 were delivered. They were 49 seaters and the scene is Stirling on the Dunfermline service shared with Midland.

180. Seen at the new Kirkcaldy bus station one of the 21 similar vehicles delivered in 1972 is seen in later life in bus livery. OMO signs are now the norm and the stand for the Setright can just be discerned through the windscreen. This pattern of mounting was developed by McMasters of Hyde, Cheshire and could also mount an Almex Model A.

181. St. Andrews Square bus station Edinburgh is the setting for Kirkcaldy bound FPE37, about to return home over the Forth Road Bridge. This was one of 16 Leopards delivered in 1974-5. The revised grille design is noteworthy in that no metal was used, the chrome finish on the grille being applied to plastic components.

182.   There were also 12 53 seat buses in 1975 and FPE57 is seen parked up in Edinburgh.   Fife took these in preference to double deckers and in fact they carried as many as one of the old lowbridge PD2s.

183.   1975 saw the arrival of Fife's first M type Leopards; these being 42 seat coaches with toilets for the Glenrothes-London service; hitherto Fife had relied on borrowed coaches in 1974 for the inauguration of this.   FPE64 is hidden away inside Kirkcaldy depot on this occasion.

184.   Only 6 Leopards reached Fife in 1977 and one of these is seen 'outside' the Kingdom in Nethergate   Dundee heading for Seagate bus station.   The arrival of the Ailsas saw less reliance on large capacity single deckers.

185. 32 more Leopard buses arrived in Fife in 1977, and the first of the batch FPE73 is seen displaying a broadside advert for Euroscot en route from Dunfermline to St. Andrews in Cupar.

186. There were 24 of these Leopards with Duple Dominant bodies delivered to Fife in 1978. Some of the batch featured Dominant II bodies having a deeper windscreen, and one of these fitted to FPE126 is seen in Kirkcaldy picking up a fare before heading north along the coast to Leven and its home depot at Aberhill.

187. The last Leopards with Y type bodies arrived in 1982 and there were 20 of these. No Leopards joined the fleet in 1981 but the 1980 deliveries accounted for 35 vehicles of which 2 were later transferred to Midland and 2 to Highland. Whilst all but the four later disposed of to other group members were 53 seaters, by virtue of having 3+2 seating on the last nine rows FPE151-4 seated 62, the largest capacity single deckers ever operated by the Scottish Bus Group. One of the 53 seaters with broadside advertising for the Glenrothes-London express service is seen leaving Glenrothes bus station on a local service.

188. The first 10, 1982 Leopard coaches featured the Alexander T type body and FPE176 finds itself outside the Sandeman Public Library in Kinnoull Street Perth in 'Cityliner' livery, when operating the Perth-Edinburgh express service. This was one of the optons being considered in 1983 before ' Citylink' was launched and involved the vehicles of each Company being painted in a distinctive livery style with 'Cityliner' logos but retaining some form of individual identity in the colour scheme used.

189. Leaving Dunfermline bus station is FPE191 on its way to St. Andrews via Glenrothes. This was a 1982 delivery and the 5 vehicles in this batch with Alexander T type bodies were the last Leopards for Fife.

190. In between the two 1982 batches of T type coaches there were the final 10 Y type bodies to be delivered to Fife on Leopard chassis. FPE184 turns out of Carnegie Drive Dunfermline on the local Townhill service.

191. Fife's first Tigers were three Duple Goldliner bodied examples new in 1983. They were in dedicated livery for the London service, and FLT3 reposes inside Kirkcaldy garage; these buses were nocturnal in their habits for most of the time, but could be 'borrowed' for other duties during the day.

192. 5 of the Tigers delivered in 1984 had Alexander TC bodies. Note the tinted glass! The two previous Tigers had Roe Doyen bodies. FLT7 is seen in Hamilton heading for Heads of Ayr and Butlins holiday camp and is possibly on loan to Central.

193. FLT11 shows the plug type entrance door fitted to this style of body. The location is also outside the 'Kingdom' - in Ayr.

194. On now to Northern territory and Northern's first Leopard, new in 1965, is seen on the BEA contract service from Aberdeen to Dyce Airport, with Aberdeen harbour in the background.

195. Northern took another six Leopards in 1967 making 10 in all, and the next batch delivered in 1968 were 53 seat buses, there being no further Leopards until 1971 when 13 arrived, also with bus bodies as exemplified by NPE21, seen here in Dundee before heading up the coast to Montrose.

196. The oil boom in the North East brought about increased business and with the launch of the Aberdeen-Corby service more vehicles were required in addition to those operating the Aberdeen-London service, which by virtue of increased motorway mileage, was operated direct. Two Leyland Leopards with Alexander M type bodies were transferred to Northern in 1975, having been new earlier in that year and NPE36 is seen here leaving Gairn Terrace, Aberdeen.

197. There were 11 Leopards for 1977, and all had Duple Dominant 1 bodies. NPE50 is seen at Aberdeen bus station on the Edinburgh service. The Citylinker board can just be discerned in the nearside of the windscreen.

198. NPE57, new to Highland in 1973, was one of 4 Leopards acquired by Northern in 1976. The 49 seat body on this bus was a replacement dating from 1976 after the original was damaged beyond repair in an accident. The location of Aberdeen bus station adjacent to the joint railway station was very convenient for interchange purposes.

199. Western SMT provided Northern with 17 more Leopards in 1983-4 and the last of these, MPE136, arrives to take up duty at Aberdeen bus station with the steeple of St. Nicholas' church in the background.

200. *Six Leyland Tigers with Duple Goldliner 46 seat bodies plus toilets arrived in 1982 for the London service. NLT1, Northern's first Tiger since the arrival of the old type chassis of the 1950s reposes at Gairn Terrace.*

201. *In 1983 Alexander phased out its Y type body and introduced the new P type and that featured in Northern's deliveries of Tigers in that year. There were 8 delivered in that year with 52 seat bodies. NBT21 was one of the 1984 deliveries which added another 7 and it is seen with the concourse of Aberdeen joint station in the background as it arrives in the bus station.*

202. *There were two of these Leyland Royal Tigers with Roe Doyen bodies new in 1984; these were Northern's first high floor coaches and were used on the London service.*

203. Leyland Nationals came to Midland in 1978. There were 5 of these A series 52 seaters, 11.3 metres long, with roof pods and MPN4 is seen on the Stirling local service from Port Street to Cornton.

204. The remaining 10 were to series B specification and were 44 seaters being 10.3 metres in length.

MPN15 is seen on a Falkirk local service.

205. The remaining Leyland Nationals arrived in two batches in 1980 and were all National 2s, 11.6 metres long without roof pods. The extra length of the National 2 was as the result of moving the radiator to the front; it was incorporated in a deeper front panel.

206. Fife took 13 National 1s in 1978 and these were 49 seaters based on the 11.3 metre shell with roof pods. FPN6 is being employed on Kirkcaldy town service.

207. Leaving Dunfermline bus station for Ballingry is FPN14. There were 12 of these National 2s new in 1979-80 with 11.6 metre bodies and no roof pods. They seated 52 and two of the batch had alternative engines, Gardner 6HLXB and Volvo TD100 for evaluation purposes.

208. Fife's last Nationals were 10 with the shorter 10.6 metre body and seats for 44. They also featured roof pods, which housed the advanced heating and ventilation system fitted to the Leyland National.

FPN34 is operating on Dunfermline local services.

209. Northern had 18 Nationals in all, delivered in 1980-1. All were National 2s, the first 12 having 106 metre bodies seating 44 and the remaining 6 had 11.6 metre bodies seating 52 and roof pods as exemplified by NPN18 seen in Fraserburgh.

210. *Fords made their first appearance in the Midland fleet in 1974 when 10 R1014 chassis with Duple Dominant coach bodies arrived. Their 41 seat bodies had folding doors as they were built to bus grant specification to allow them to qualify for that grant; indeed they had to spend some of their working lives on stage services. Not so for MT4 which is far away from home in the Yorkshire seaside resort of Scarborough.*

211. *The next deliveries of Fords included 8 R1114s with Alexander Y type bus bodies, but for 1975 there were 3 with Duple Dominant 45 seat coach bodies like MT21 seen here. The use of the destination aperture to advise of 'Pay as you enter' means that stickers have to be resorted to when on stage carriage work, which is keeping this bus gainfully employed as it leaves Glasgow's Buchanan bus station, opened in December 1976.*

212. *The Alexander bodied Fords all had AYS type bodies and Larbert's MT41 is one of the 53 seat variety, others being 45 seaters. Further Ford buses of the same types were delivered up to 1979 but earlier batches were being withdrawn by 1982. It was found that the heavier Alexander Y type bodywork caused problems with the Ford chassis.*

213. *Northern however found the Ford R series chassis most suited to its needs and took its first 15 in 1971. One of these NT15 is seen in Fraserburgh about to head out to St. Combs, a fishing village once served by a branch railway from Fraserburgh.*

214. *The first 10 Fords delivered to Northern in 1973 were unusual in that they were 41 seat coaches with Alexander Y type bodies, as exemplified by NT58 seen here in Fraserburgh. There were also another 10 45 seat and 5 53 seat buses.*

215. *To complete our illustration of the three types of Alexander bodied Fords we see one of the 1974 deliveries NT81, again in Fraserburgh, this time a 45 seater.*

216. Northern had also taken some Duple bodied Fords in 1974, but turned to that bodybuilder for all of the 1976 deliveries. There were two varieties as seen on this page. The first four had 45 seat Dominant 1 bodies as seen on NT136.

217. The remainder were 49 seaters on R1114 chassis, and NT147 is seen in Aberdeen. There were 14 in total.

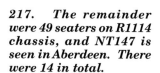

218. Whilst for the 1977 deliveries Alexander bodies returned, there were 7 of these 53 seat buses which employed the Duple Dominant body shell, but finished to a reduced specification, fitted with bus type seats, reduced trim, and opening ventilators. The last of the batch is seen in Aberdeen with one of Grampian's AEC Swifts with Alexander W type bodies new in 1971. Northern's last Fords arrived in 1980.

219. Although Northern had put its faith in the Ford Motor Co. it was found that the Fords were not giving the length of service first expected of them.   Two vehicles were acquired in 1983. NA1 used a Volvo B57 chassis lengthened by Volvo (GB) Ltd., and was a 53 seater. The engine was at the front as per the Ailsas, and indeed was the same TD70 unit; the choice of a turbocharged engine meant that. like the Ailsa double decker, the engine took up less space for the power developed.   This bus received the last Alexander Y type body built.

220.   The other vehicle was a Dennis Lancet SD511 chassis, again with Alexander body. The mid mounted Perkins V8-540 engine gave a high chassis height and thus the body is noticeably taller.

221. ND1 was followed in 1984 by 5 more Lancets but these had Alexander P type bodies. ND2 is seen in Aberdeen and these vehicles too had taller bodies - compare with the Leyland Tiger in plate 201..

222. Fife was not that fond of Fords, taking 10 45 seat Duple Dominant bodied coaches in 1974-5. Here FT3 is employed on stage carriage work, obviously on the Leven to Edinburgh service if the stickers can be trusted.

223. The only other 7 Fords were 53 seat buses with Alexander bodies. Here FT16 leaves Cupar. All Fife's Fords were soon disposed of, the coaches going to Highland in 1979 and this batch of buses bar one in 1982.

224. Before 1961 Bedfords were to be found in Alexanders fleet in some number, but at the time of the split there were only 32 in stock, all in the Midland and Northern areas. Fife took delivery of 4 VAS1 chassis in 1962, three with Duple Bella Vista coach bodies as seen on FW1 parked at Glasgow's Dundas Street bus station and a fourth with Duple Midland bus body similar to the Midland example illustrated opposite. All four were disposed of in 1972, FW1 running for three English independent operators.

225. One of Midland's coach examples also new in 1962, MW264 is seen operating the Glens & Bens public tour. These 29 seaters took over the extended tour work once performed by the Bedford OB and SB coaches.

226. Midland also ran one VAS1 with Duple Midland 30 seat bus body and it is seen in Oban outside the railway station. MW266 passed to SMT, the Bedford dealers who of course before nationalisation were part of the SMT group as was Alexanders, in 1972 and it is not known to where it was disposed of.

227. Midland took more Bedfords in 1967; there were 15 VAM5 coaches with Duple Viceroy bodies seating 45. MW284 is seen at the Station Hotel, Perth, also owned at that time by the British Transport Commission, on an extended tour, duties which these vehicles had taken over from the SBG type Bedfords new to Alexanders in 1956. Bedfords, being lightweights, tended to have around a 10 year life in the Alexanders fleets.

228. One of Northern's two VAS1 buses, NW265, is seen here, it was new in 1964, there being one more which was new in 1962. Northern also received three VAS1 coaches in 1962.

229. Northern took a further five Bedfords in 1968, three of which were VAS5 chassis with Duple Vista 2S bodies; there being a revised window layout, front panel, and trim on these later examples.

230. Northern took 2 VAM70 chassis in 1968 and a further 4 in 1970. The 1968 deliveries including NW272 had Duple Viceroy bodies. These were Northern's last Bedfords, the future choice being Fords; indeed two of the 1972 Fords had Duple Viceroy bodies but of an improved style.

231.   Drivers have to be trained, and at one time it was essential that a PSV licence for double deckers with manual gearbox was obtained as this permitted the holder to drive any kind of PSV.   MRD53, seen here, became Midland's driving trainer ML274 in 1974. It was painted in a yellow and maroon livery.

232.   NRB222 became Driving trainer N226DT in May 1977 and is seen in Aberdeen making a left turn into Union Street.

233.   Northern used former MRD201 as a driving trainer in the 1970s; it had been acquired along with 5 others from Midland in 1979.   The stairs were removed and this allowed the instructor to be positioned directly behind the driver. The scene is Union Terrace Aberdeen with 'Rabbie Burns' in the background.

234. Fife inherited this 1939 TS8 converted into a tow wagon in 1960. It had been bus P551.

235. Northern used this Leyland recovery vehicle based at Aberdeen for the big jobs, most larger garages retaining a 'tow wagon' for dealing with minor emergencies and breakdowns. It was based on an Leyland 'Bull' chassis coming to Alexanders from an unidentified owner via Millburn Motors.

236. Dunfermline's tow wagon started life as one of Alexanders Craven Bodied Guy Arabs in 1948 and was fitted with this home built body at the Gallatown works in 1964.

237. The next generation of tow wagons can be seen here. This is Midland's conversion of a 1965 Leyland Leopard executed in 1980. The front of the original body has been retained but the wheelbase has been shortened. The livery was still 'SMT red' and ivory. The location is Larbert Road garage.

238. This is Northern's version of the same seen at Gairn Terrace, Aberdeen. There was also a workbench behind the seats provided for the crew inside the body, with equipment to enable 'on the road repairs' to be made to vehicle fuel systems etc.

239. This vehicle started life operating with Wallace Arnold, Leeds, passing to Carson Dunvegan, Skye in 1967. It went to MacBraynes in 1970 and was passed on to Highland Omnibuses who didn't operate it. Alexanders Northern acquired the vehicle shortly afterwards and it was not operated but used as a training vehicle to instruct crews in the new decimal coinage.

240. We now move on to the absorbed operators of the 1960s. Carmichael of Glenboig (Trading as 'Highland') operated this one Leyland PD3. It had been built as a 'stock' delivery for Millburn Motors in 1962, the body having been built at the end of a batch for Glasgow Corporation. Acquired by Carmichael in the same year it is seen in his red and cream livery. On takeover in 1966 it passed to Midland as MRB282 and was the only ex 'Highland' double decker to be used by Midland. It became the only highbridge 'decker on Midlands books until the Ailsas arrived.

241. Carmichael bought two Leyland Leopards with Alexander bodies in 1961. They were 45 seat buses and Midland repainted them in coach livery at first but later, like Midland's own Tiger Cubs. - they acquired bus livery. Midland never operated any new Leopards with other than Y type bodies, the vehicle shown here becoming MPE84.

242. MNL19 also ran in the Carmichael fleet. It was a Albion Aberdonian with Plaxton 41 seat body new to Smith of Wigan in 1957. They didn't keep it long and it had two other owners before arriving at Glenboig in 1964. It lasted with Midland until 1972.

243. Seen in Coatbridge is MPF3, one of 5 Leyland Worldmasters new to Glasgow Corporation in 1957, all of which were acquired by Carmichael in 1965. Seen in full Midland livery with Cumbernauld depot plates this reminds us that Carmichael's Glenboig premises were closed in late 1967 when a new garage was opened in Cumbernauld.

244. Carmichael bought 4 Willowbrook bodied Leopards in 1963/4 and these became MPE85-88 on acquisition by Midland. The last new vehicle purchased by 'Highland' after becoming MPE88 is seen here, again in Coatbridge.

245. MPD275 was new to Carmichael in 1960. It was a Leyland Tiger Cub with Duple Midland 41 seat coach body. It is seen in Cumbernauld in Bluebird livery.

246. Strachans Deeside Omnibus Service were taken over by Northern on 3rd may 1965, and involved 12 vehicles, 7 of which were Fodens. NF1 shown here was new to Campbell of Aberdeen (owned later by the SCWS - Scottish Co-operative Wholesale Society) and passed to Strachans in 1957 when it was 10 years old. All the Fodens had gone by the end of 1967 but survived long enough for some to have Northern fleet numbers applied.

247. NAC51 was luckier, lasting until 1973. It is seen here in full Northern livery; when new it would have been seen in the primrose and orange of Wallace Arnold of Leeds, from whence it passed to Strachans in 1963. The scene is Aberdeen bus station, and the curvaceous Duple bodywork contrasts with the angularity of NAC125.

248. Burnetts Motors of Mintlaw succumbed in January 1967, and they operated 14 vehicles including this Burlingham Seagull bodied AEC Reliance new in 1957. It lasted until 1973. It was common practice for many independent operators to buy new coaches and second-hand buses for stage work.

249. WPT136 became NAC8 and was new to Shaw, Byers Green, in 1957, arriving in the north east in 1962. It was an AEC Reliance with Plaxton 41 seat coach body. Northern ran it until 1973.

250. Burnett's Double deckers were 4 in number, all AEC Regents acquired from City of Oxford Motor Services. NRC23 had a Park Royal 53 seat lowbridge body and was new in 1950 passing to Burnetts in 1964. It is seen in full Northern livery at Mintlaw and ran as such until 1972.

251. NRC25 had a Weymann body and the platform doors were added by Burnetts. Following repaints by Northern the ex Burnetts vehicles looked very smart - in the latter-day Burnett era they were getting a little tatty!

252. Simpsons of Rosehearty were taken over in December 1966, and seen parked at their former premises is NRC1, An ex London Transport RT new in 1947 as RT157 and acquired by Simpsons, along with 3 other examples, from Browns Blue of Markfield Leicestershire in April 1963 at their dispersal sale. The other 3 had gone by the time of the takeover, but this one lasted until the end of 1968 still in Simpsons livery. The author remembers being very surprised at seeing this very vehicle in Perth whilst awaiting another ex London bus, a wartime Guy, passing through Bridgend Perth in May 1963.

253. KGG711 was new to David MacBrayne, Glasgow in 1952 arriving at Rosehearty by 1965. It is seen here before the takeover in Mealmarket Street, Aberdeen, a departure point for a number of services before the bus station was opened. It was an AEC Regal IV with Roe 44 seat body. It had gone by 1968 but did receive Northern fleet number NAB13.

254. Also in Mealmarket Street can be found the last new bus bought by Simpson, a Ford R192 with Plaxton Panorama body. It survived until 1976 by which time Northern were embarking on large purchases of new Fords; one wonders whether the operation of 4 Fords from Simpsons had any influence?

255. Simpsons replaced the ex Browns Blue RTs and other older double deckers with 8 Leyland PS1s new to Yorkshire Traction or County Motors as single deckers. All were rebuilt by Yorkshire Traction to take double deck bodies by Roe in 1955/6 and they were bought by Simpson in 1965. Two are seen at Rosehearty, still in Simpsons livery but with Northern fleet plates attached.

256. NRA106 looks very smart repainted in Northern livery at Fraserburgh. The application of cream round the upper deck windows was unique to these vehicles. It ran thus until 1971; an influx of second-hand double deckers from Western SMT meant the end for these handsome vehicles.

257. Simpsons other 1965 acquisition is seen in Northern days and livery as NT7, still allocated to Rosehearty. Alexanders not only took over Strachans, Simpsons and Burnetts vehicles they also inherited their insert Setright machines; it is pleasing to note that unlike most of the vehicles most of these have survived and the author has one of each in his collection.

258. Mitchell of Luthermuir was taken over in October 1967 and 11 vehicles were involved. This is NT9, a Ford 570E with Burlingham 41 seat coach body. It was new to Whittles of Highley in 1959, and passed via two other owners, to Mitchells in 1965. It was sold in 1971. This style of Burlingham body was not the most attractive of their 'Seagull' range!

259. More at home in Northern livery is NPD15, a Leyland Tiger Cub with Alexander coach body seated as a 45 seat bus, new to Hutchison Overtown in 1954, later passing to Gibson of Moffat. Mitchells bought it in 1967 just before the takeover and it ran until 1972.

260. Two more of Mitchells fleet are seen in Montrose, with SPT69, a Guy Arab LUF with Weymann body new in 1955 to Northern General; this became NGA1 and was operated by Alexanders Northern until 1969. Mitchells bought it in 1966. NPD13 was one of two ex Western Welsh Tiger Cubs bought in 1966, and the only one operated by Mitchell. NPD14 was taken to Aberdeen straight after the takeover and prepared for service by Northern.

Alexander's Ticket equipment

Since the first volume of this book was written further information about ticket equipment has come to light. The first Setrights, around 150 machines, were installed at Stirling, Larbert Road and Stepps in 1931. The general conversion to Setrights took place from 1935, these replacing most of the other early 'narrow' Setrights and punch tickets.

The SMB or 'speed' machine which went into production in 1948 in due course replaced 'Ultimates' in Stirling and Falkirk. The nature of local services in these areas was such that vehicles and crews often had to undertake 'out of town' journeys as well and this caused problems, so the 'Speed' was the answer. The machines were however, more versatile due to the wider fare range and from 1955, they replaced all types of machines, the facility being available on the 'speeds' to issue and cancel insert type returns and weeklies through a slot in the front.

Kirkcaldy and Perth soldiered on with the Ultimates, Perth even having six 6 unit machines for the 107 (37) Cherrybank/Scone service from 1964. A previous trial of 12 6 unit machines in May 1957 lasted only until December 1960 when these and 108 5 unit machines were withdrawn, from Stirling and Falkirk. Kirkcaldy retained some TIM machines longer than anybody else for standby duties and these were last recorded in use in 1963, after a fare increase. A few TIMs also soldiered on in the Northern area, in Montrose and Peterhead.

Kirkcaldy went over to 'Speeds' entirely in 1963/4, and this left Perth using up the stocks of everybody else's Ultimate tickets. Ultimates were eventually withdrawn from Perth in December 1968 in favour of Setright Speeds.

The Northern area inherited the majority of the remaining Insert machines. Due to the fare range required on some long distance services some Setright Speeds were delivered to the Midland and Fife Companies in the mid 1960s with a fare range from 0-39/11 in 1d steps. The fare was shown on the ticket as fare/plus.

Decimalisation saw the elimination of most of the remaining Insert Setrights by Setright Speeds, although Almex machines had been tried in various locations at various times. All machines delivered to the three companies after 1965 were of the improved Mk. II design and large numbers of these machines were in position to effect the changeover to decimal coinage from 15th February, 1971, most of the remaining Mk1 machines being 'kit' converted beforehand. The level of fare increases in the 1970s caused the Scottish Bus Group to request the development of an extended range SMB by Setright Registers the which Setrights called the MkIIE and SBG Companies incorrectly called the MkIII. This had three fare indexes and could cope with fares from 0-£9.99. Setrights continued to be the predominant method of fare collection until the mid 1980s, all companies retaining manually operated machines mounted on stands for One Man Operation. Solomatics were tried without success, and there were also trials with motor driven Setrights but these were not universally adopted. Electronic equipment has gradually ousted the Setrights since the early 1980s, Fife being the first to introduce Wayfarer 1s in 1984, Midland and Northern following in 1985.

Working Practices

As weekly tickets were available on certain services which normally used other types of ticket equipment (i.e. TIM or Ultimate), it was normal practice to arrange for a Setright to be used on the Monday morning for the issue of 10 or 12 Journey tickets and revert to the normal machine for the rest of the week. This sometimes applied on the Perth/Pitcairngreen service, RN stores buses and elsewhere. Setright machines on stands were held at all Offices for tours and weekly bookings.

Every year, a statistical survey was carried out. This involved the issue of special tickets. Whilst the Setright issues were normally Green Single/Yellow ½d Surcharge/Pink Return; the statistical issues were White Single/Blue ½d Surcharge/Orange Return. Each week a different fare was selected and the special tickets issued only for that fare. Most of the speed machines had a statistical counter which eliminated the need for these tickets eventually.

Special Insert tickets were also issued for vehicles crossing the Tay Road Bridge as a toll was levied per passenger. These were buff return and orange single, there were also special 10/12 journey issues.

With the advent of Speed machines, Return and weekly tickets were still issued through a special slot in the front of the machines; this practice continued insofar as returns were concerned until the early 80s when only weeklies were issued therefrom, and the returns issued from the normal roll. From D day when Speeds became universal, the DMSSP lettering was omitted from further printings of insert tickets. Setright Speed rolls were by GNP.

On Perth City Services, special Bell Punch style tickets printed by GNP were provided for the statistical survey being cancelled by a small Bakelite punch mounted on the machine strap. Records show that Alexanders bought 288 of these from the Bell Punch Co on an unspecified date.

On routes also operated by Scottish Omnibuses, or other SBG companies, the Return ticket was retained by the conductor and an Exchange ticket issued. Strange to say this practice did not occur when vehicles of two Alexander Companies shared the same route after 1961!

Other special Insert tickets appeared in the 1970s and early 1980s; day out tickets, and special 10 and 12 journey issues. The use of Almex machines for statistical purposes in connection with Scotmap etc. seems to have been the reason for each garage having a small allocation by the early 1980s. These machines, having an audit roll, could provide extensive audit and traffic information.

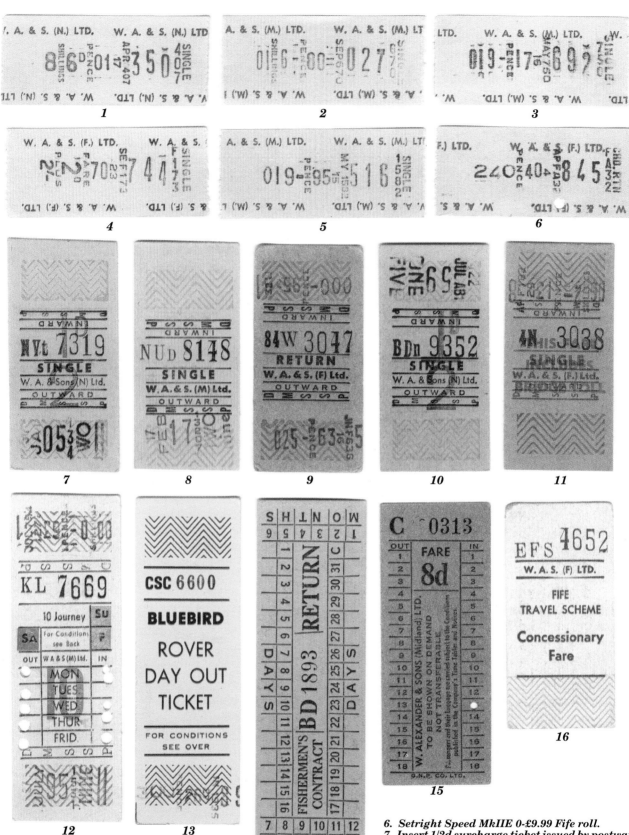

Key to ticket illustrations

1. *Setright Speed MkI pre decimal single Alexanders Northern Roll.*
2. *Setright Speed Mk1 decimal kit converted format before D day Midland roll..*
3. *Setright Speed Mk1 decimal kit converted format after D day Midland roll..*
4. *Setright Speed Mk1 pre decimal extended range machine fares 0-39/11d Fife roll..*
5. *Setright Speed MkII later model Midland roll..*
6. *Setright Speed MkIIE 0-£9.99 Fife roll.*
7. *Insert 1/2d surcharge ticket issued by postwar insert Setright LRD machine 134.*
8. *Insert Single ticket issued by postwar insert Setright LRD machine 13207.*
9. *Insert Return ticket issued through Setright Speed MkII slot and cancelled by same.*
10. *Insert 1/2d census ticket issued by prewar insert Setright register AB1.*
11. *Insert Single ticket issued through Setright Speed MkI for Tay Bridge crossing.*
12. *Insert 10 Journey Weekly.*
13. *Insert Rover day out ticket. 1970s.*
14. *Fishermen's Contract Ticket - Alexanders (Northern).*
15. *8d punch ticket for census on Perth City Services.*
16. *Fife Concessionary fare insert ticket.*
Tickets 1-16 are all printed by GNP.

17. Bell Punch. 2d Ultimate ticket block style issued on Perth City Services.
18. Bell Punch. 3d Ultimate ticket Phase 'A' issued on Perth City Services.
19. Bell Punch. 2d Ultimate ticket Phase 'B' issued on Perth City Services.
20. Bell Punch. 4d Ultimate ticket Phase 'C' issued on Perth City Services.
21. Bell Punch. 9d Ultimate ticket Phase 'C' manilla paper (1000 per roll) issued on Perth City Services.
22. Bell Punch 3 1/2d phase 'A' Ultimate ticket printed for Fife but used on Perth City Services.
23. Bell Punch 2 1/2d phase 'C' Ultimate ticket printed for Fife but used on Perth City Services.
24. Scholars Season Ticket.
25. Fife Wayfarer 1 ticket.
26. Almex Model A ticket.
27. Emergency duplex book ticket.

Liveries

Following the division of the Alexander empire into three, the azure blue and ivory livery continued to be used on all vehicles for the first eight months or so. The only visible differences were the alteration to the legal ownership and where vehicles had been repainted, the existing fleetname transfers were modified to show "& Sons (— —) Ltd. instead of "& Sons Ltd." to use up stocks.

1962 saw the three companies take on distinctive identities.

Midland

Walter Alexander & Sons (Midland) Ltd inherited the blue and ivory of the original Company. By 1961 however the use of dark blue had been discontinued and there were two basic schemes in use for single deckers, coach or 'Bluebird' livery, and bus livery. The coach livery used ivory as the predominant colour and to this was applied blue in varying degrees. Service coaches or to be more precise, those termed 'dual purpose' tended to have blue roofs and flashes, whilst touring coaches had ivory as the main colour with only blue applied to the waistband. Buses were predominantly blue with ivory window surrounds and waistbands. A script style of 'Midland' fleetname was adopted and in the case of older vehicles this was applied as a large transfer on the blue of the side panels, whilst newer single deckers and coaches had it applied on the waistband. Coaches continued to use the 'Bluebird' emblem.

Double deckers continued in a predominantly azure blue scheme with black mudguards and varying number of ivory bands. Whilst it had been the practice until 1961 to have only one ivory band on lowbridge double deckers some of these began to have the area above the lower deck windows in this colour also. Full ivory lining out continued to be applied to the tween decks panels; the advertisement panels if not used also being ivory. The ivory bands were edged in black and there was also an ivory line below the lower deck windows.

Some of the Leyland PD3s had the whole of the upper deck side panels painted ivory in 1963, but this scheme did not last and was superseded with one where three ivory bands were applied. Some of the Albion Lowlanders when new only had one ivory band above the lower deck windows but another below the upper deck windows was soon applied.

The original delivery of Daimler Fleetlines were in traditional livery with two ivory bands, the lower one being swept up over the cab, entrance and windscreen area. The second delivery featured ivory roofs and window surrounds but this style didn't last and all were soon in standard livery. Double deckers were again turned out in the 1963 style with the 1980 Fleetline deliveries, but the white lining out was dropped with the appearance of the rear engined double deckers. Alexander Coachbuilders continued to apply the black lining but the ECW VRTs came with none at all, and in due course this became the norm as a cost saving exercise. Alexanders vehicles were all still brush painted in coach enamel.

The appearance of the Alexander R type body brought further changes and the Metrobuses had an ivory area around and above the lower deck windows. The vehicles employed in the trials of 1981 including the prototype Olympian had the upper deck side panels in ivory also.

Service buses from 1967 also began to appear with ivory window surrounds and this scheme was also applied to coaches which were being cascaded onto service work, as had been the practice for many years. From 1978 the lower side panels or skirt became blue on coaches and this was the scheme applied to the new Alexander T type bodies.

From 1965 the script fleetname gave way to one which revived the style of the original W. Alexander & Sons Ltd style but with W. Alexander & Sons Midland Ltd. in full, the Midland part of the name being prominent. In 1968 a sans serif style using lower case lettering was adopted. The corporate "Midland Scottish" fleetname with saltire appeared in 1978, but there had been one anomany before that, the use of "Midland-Bluebird" on the 1967 Duple bodied Bedfords. It was only applied to this class of vehicle and went with the adoption of the corporate image in 1978.

Fife

Fife adopted Ayres Red as their main colour in 1962, this shade being the same as used by the Tilling group companies who used red. In general terms, the styles used could be said to follow those used by Midland, but one anomaly was the use of an overall red livery for double deckers. Fife discontinued the use of white and black lining out earlier than Midland. The transfers from Central

SMT and Western SMT saw the Lodekkas and Lowlanders enter service in some cases in their original livery with or without fleetnames old or new! A broad ivory band appeared on some of the Ailsas but was soon eliminated, but the final double deck livery until 1985 was all red with one ivory band above the lower deck windows.

Service buses were all red, with ivory flashes or waistband. Some batches of new single deckers had red window surrounds, others ivory, and coaches tended to have ivory roofs when new, gaining red ones when cascaded. The practice of repainting coaches downgraded to bus work in bus livery continued.

The Alexander T type coaches featured red skirts, and the late 1970s saw the appearance of advertising slogans on the side panels of some single deck buses resulting in the appearance of a wide ivory band below the windows and a red skirt. Duple bodied coaches offered the most variety, the red being applied to suit the style of trim.

Fife used the script style of fleetname right up until 1978 when it took on the corporate identity.

Northern

The most radical of the new liveries was that of Northern, said to be inspired by that of Newcastle Corporation, although the brown wheels didn't last beyond the first few repaints. Northern did more experimentation than the other two Companies which involved the amounts of Yellow and white used. On single deckers an overall yellow with ivory flashes was tried, whilst coaches simply had the Bluebird livery with yellow substituting for blue. The final scheme for buses involved ivory roofs and flashes, black mudguards, and yellow side panels. Dual purpose saloons used coach livery. From 1977 when coaches were cascaded an all over yellow livery with ivory waistband was adopted. This scheme was also applied to the Duple Dominant E type bodies which made them look odd when compared with the equivalent coaches with the same body shell.

Double deckers were tried in various schemes before Northern settled on limiting the ivory to the lower deck window surrounds and above.

Black lining out in the style of the old white lines was applied at first to the upper deck side panels but this was later dropped. The Albion Lowlanders when new had ivory roof and upper deck window surrounds. The prototype Olympian retained its Midland style demonstration livery with the blue repainted yellow, but most Olympians followed standard practice with the ivory restricted to the lower deck window surrounds and above.

The script fleetname in gold was used from 1962 until 1970 when it became black, and a black underlined gill sans lower case fleetname was adopted in 1971, surviving until the onslaught of corporate identity in 1978.

In 1983 local services in the Aberdeen area were combined under the Grampian Scottish fleetname, a version of the corporate style being adopted, and vehicles were painted in a green and cream livery related to that used by Grampian Regional Transport.

London Coaches

The Alexander Companies didn't get involved in express or overnight services to London, starting initially with feeders into the existing network provided by Western SMT from Glasgow and Scottish Omnibuses from Edinburgh. The 1975 Fife M type coaches ran for a short time in red and ivory, but in 1976 a blue and white corporate livery featuring a large saltire emblem and Scottish fleetname was adopted for all SBG services to London. This was later enhanced by the application of smaller corporate fleetnames of the owning Company applied on the front panel.

Scottish Citylink

The deregulation of express services and increasing competition from the fledgling Stagecoach and other operators saw the network of long distance express services promoted under the Scottish Citylink name. Extensive advertising and the application of a startling yellow and two tone blue livery launched the new identity on 1st October 1983. It was usual for vehicles to be reseated with reclining seats for express services, and former London coaches were also employed on medium distance express routes. Scottish Citylink survived the 1985 reorganisation, also taking on board the London operations, and new liveries were adopted in 1991, but with the privatisation process since then it has operated as a separate company contract hiring coaches from not only the former SBG Companies but independents as well.

C1. P682 sits in the sun at the top of Killermont Street Glasgow in full Midland bus livery.

C2. Midland's Royal Tigers as exemplified by MPC65 ran for a while in this reversed livery but finished their days back in the original style.

C3. The 1961 Coaches were painted in what was the standard coach livery with azure blue waistbands.

MPD223 is seen at Larbert Road.

C4. MT14 shows the latter-day bus livery with lower case fleetnames and is obviously needing a visit to Brown Street to have a scrape on the roof repaired. It is seen at Kirkintilloch garage.

C5. MRB250, one of the 1961 rebuilds, looks as if it is straight from the paintshop in this post 1968 shot. Note that the white lining has now been dropped but the black edging to the ivory bands is still being applied. All the lining out was done by hand and one reason for the economy in dropping same was the shortage of skilled labour in the early 1970s.

C6. MRD115 displays the standard livery for Lodekkas and also the fleetname style used from 1965-68.

C7. Perth's MRT15 shows the style in which these VRTs came from ECW with no black lining at all.

It is seen at Larbert Road, but whether the visit is to repair the accident damage visible to the front nearside or to await despatch to Eastern National is not known. One thing is certain however, that the author remembers how this vehicle got its dent but discretion prevents its revelation.

C8. The Fleetlines were lined out in black however, and MRF31 shows that the Alexander fleet still looked very smart as it awaits further work at Milngavie Garage in the 1970s.

Fleet Statistics - May 1961

		Fife	Midland	Northern	Total
A	AEC Regal	––	15	72	87
A	AEC Regal III	––	––	6	6
AB	AEC Regal III	––	10	––	10
AC	AEC Reliance/Monocoach	––	94	112	206
AL	Albion Valkyrie		––	1*	1
BA	Albion Victor	5	––	––	5
C	Commer Commando		9	––	9
D	Daimler CVD6 single deck.		37	4	41
E	Bristol LS	20	––	––	20
G	Guy Arab single deck	79	22	––	101
GA	Guy Arab LUF	20	––	––	20
K	Leyland Cheetah	8	3	––	11
N	Albion Nimbus	––	15	––	15
NL	Albion Aberdonian	5	1	17	23
P	Leyland Tiger TS7/8	40	82	49	171
PA	Leyland Tiger PS1	45	94	60	199
PB	Leyland Tiger OPS2	10	6	4	20#
PC	Leyland Royal Tiger	11	57	16	84
PD	Leyland Tiger Cub	57	137	10	204
R	Leyland Titan TD4/5/7	12	65	16	93
RA	Leyland Titan PD1	––	48	26	74
RB	Leyland Titan PD2	26	58	23	107
	Leyland Titan PD3	––	57	19	76
RC	AEC Regent III	––	20	2*	22
RD	Bristol Lodekka LD6G	80	72	––	152
RO	Guy Arab 1/11 double deck	73	37	––	110
	Guy Arab III double deck	25	––	––	25
	Daimler CWA6 double deck	––	3	10*	13
W	Bedford.	––	25	7	32
	TOTAL	**516**	**967**	**454**	**1937**

Notes * Vehicles taken over from James Sutherland, Peterhead.

\# 17 of these rebuilt to PS1 standard during 1961.

Fleet Statistics March 1985

Midland

MPE	Leyland Leopard	285
MPN	Leyland National	39
MPT	Leyland Tiger	37
MRA	Volvo-Ailsa D/d	13
MRF	Daimler Fleetline	70
MRM	Metrobus	107
MSE	Seddon Pennine	30
MT	Ford	24

Fife

FLT	Leyland Tiger	11
FPE	Leyland Leopard	141
FPN	Leyland National	35
FRA	Volvo-Ailsa D/d	76
FRF	Daimler Fleetline	29
FRN	Leyland Atlantean	10
FRO	Leyland Olympian	10

Northern

NA	Volvo-Ailsa B57	1
NBT	Leyland Tiger	15
NCT	Leyland Tiger	12
NEC	Leyland Tiger	1
NCM	Metrobus	7
ND	Dennis Lancet	6
NDM	Metrobus	2
NLO	Olympian	60
NLT	Leyland Tiger	6
NPE	Leyland Leopard	102
NPN	Leyland National	18
NRF	Daimler Fleetline	21
NRT	Leyland Royal Tiger	2
NT	Ford	90

Totals	605	312	343

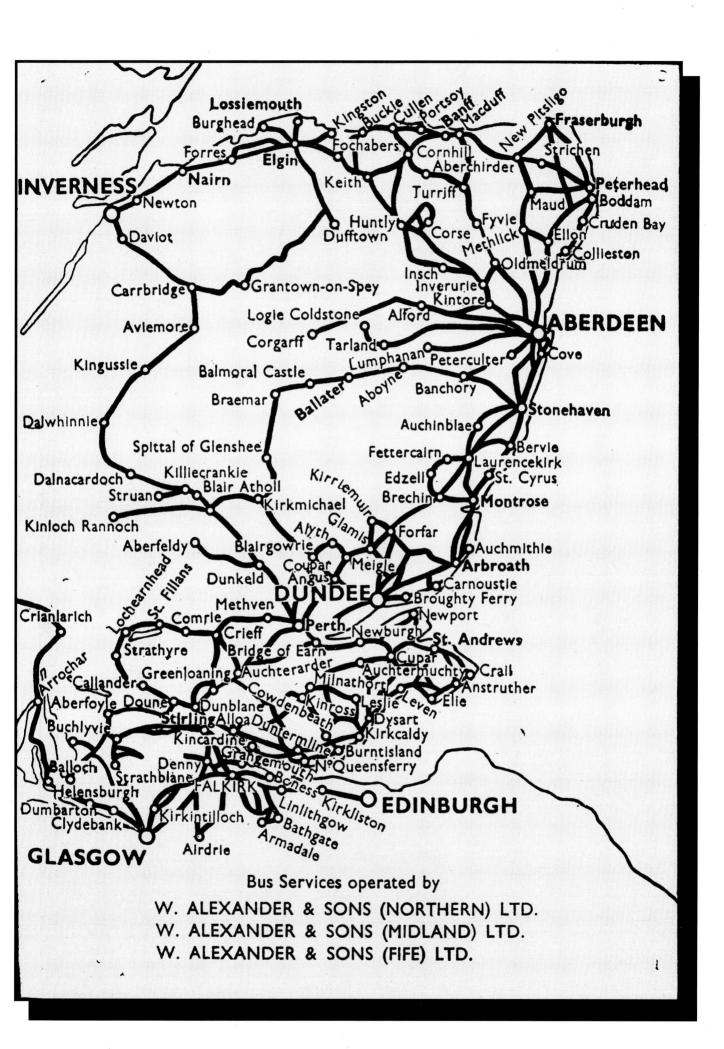

Bus Services operated by

W. ALEXANDER & SONS (NORTHERN) LTD.
W. ALEXANDER & SONS (MIDLAND) LTD.
W. ALEXANDER & SONS (FIFE) LTD.

C9. Fife's bus livery as applied to the FE class is seen on FE6 parked in the works yard at Kirkcaldy obviously awaiting attention to some accident damage.

C10. FAC9 displays the livery applied to dual purpose vehicles, expressly some of the 1962 deliveries.

C11. Coach livery is displayed on FPE32 seen in Edinburgh.

C12. FE33 is seen painted in 'London' livery. This vehicle was acquired from Scottish Omnibuses early in 1978. It was new in 1966 as XA168 and came to Fife with XA169 for use on the Glenrothes-London service. They had 38 seats and a toilet.

C13. Fife's RO505 displays the original interpretation of double deck livery; the Ayres red was a lighter shade than the 'SMT' red used previously on Kirkcaldy town service buses.

C14. One of the ex Central SMT Lodekkas FRD104 has been repainted in the simplified livery introduced for double deckers in the early 1970s.

C15. A Northern Counties bodied Albion Lowlander new to Central in 1962 has been repainted in Fife livery.

C16. The Fife Ailsas featured an all over red scheme with only the tween-decks band to break it up. FRA8 is shown here.

261. Glasgow sported two bus stations used by Alexanders. Here RB251 dives into the gloom of Killermont Street Bus Station. Of note are the slogan and garter on the rear panel. The advert for Red Tape Whisky is unusual - most Alexanders double deckers at one time advertised Askit Powders or Bells Whisky in this space.

262. Just round the corner was Dundas Street Bus Station where a collection of ex Lawson vehicles are seen along with AC35, a Park Royal Monocoach performing a shortworking on the Glasgow-Dunfermline service.

263. Glasgow's two former bus stations were swept away in the redevelopment which followed the closure of Buchanan Street railway station in 1966. Much negotiation took place with Glasgow City Council regarding compensation for the two sites and a replacement. This came about in December 1975. Midland's MLO1 is seen at one of the stances.

264. London coaches receive maintenance at Aberdeen's Gairn Terrace depot.

265. Five ex Western SMT PD2s line up at Fraserburgh to await further journeys which at one time would have been the business of James Sutherland, Simpsons or Burnetts.

266. Montrose garage after the Mitchell's takeover sees two ex Mitchell vehicles evident in this view.

C17. AC15, a Reliance new in 1954 displays the livery normally associated with dual purpose vehicles when seen in Arbroath in this post 1971 view showing the lower case fleetname.

C18. Bus livery was more usual on Reliances and Monocoaches, and NAC2 displays this along with the second style of script fleetname in black.

C19. One of Northern's only batch of Alexander bodied Ford coaches shows off coach livery with underlined fleetname and bluebird decals.

C20. NT170, one of Northern's many Ford buses shows the bus livery as applied to the AY type body.

C21. The curvaceous lines of NRC22 are seen as the sun makes Northern's scheme as finally adopted for double deckers gleam!

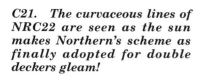

C22. The black lining out on the upper deck side panels was later dropped as seen on this view of ex Sutherland NRA101 taken in Aberdeen.

C23.   NRF21 is seen in Aberdeen with a TSB advert which also shows the route of the cross town service from Dyce to Cults. It was one of 8 new in 1978 and these proved to be Northern's only new Fleetlines.

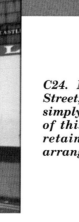

C24. NRO1 turns into Castle Street, Aberdeen. Northern simply painted the blue parts of this vehicle yellow so it retained its unique colour arrangements.

Miscellania

Destination Displays.

All three Companies continued to use the pattern used before 1961, with a single destination display and three track number blind. On single deckers these were side by side, on double deckers the number blinds were above the destination, and the trend with double deckers continued the use of both screens in a triangular surround. More recent single deck vehicles tended to have the number blinds on the offside to make alteration easier when OMO was in vogue.

Uniforms.

The traditional style of uniforms continued in use by all three companies until 1970. Cap badges were of the same style as hitherto but with the full company name eg. W. Alexander & Sons (Fife) Ltd., instead of W. Alexander & Sons Ltd. In 1970 new uniforms were issued and these were of simplified design, with detail differences between the three Companies and much less piping than before. The Corporate image adopted by the Scottish Bus Group in 1978 saw the introduction of new style lightweight uniforms in a blue/grey colour with American style caps (not liked by the crews) and badges which reflected the new Corporate fleetname with Saltaire emblem. It has to be said that standards of appearance declined in the 1970s, and were not helped by the new uniform styles.

Bibliography & Further Reading.

Readers will find that some of the books listed are out of print but are available second-hand from good suppliers. In researching and writing this book primary sources have, in the main, been consulted and previously published works used to check facts etc afterwards..

British Bus Fleets 22. Scottish Bus Group. Ian Allan 1965.

Booth, Gavin...Alexander Coachbuilders, Transport Publishing Company 1980

Brown, Stewart J....Alexanders Buses, Roadliner Transport Books 1984.

Grieves, Robert...Alexander Album, XS Publications 1978.

Fleet Histories PL2, PL3 and PM6, The PSV Circle and Omnibus Society.

Major Bus Operators - Scotland. Capital Transport 1985.

Bus Handbook 10 - Scotland capital Transport 1992

Keith A. Jenkinson .Best Bus, The Final years of the Scottish Bus Group..Autobus Review Publications 1991.

Buses Illustrated and Buses

Classic Bus

Company Time-tables, notices and handbooks.

Annual reports of the Transport Holding Company and the Scottish Transport Group.

Photographic Credits.

Thanks are again due to all those who have provided prints for this volume. Again if any photographs are incorrectly attributed we apologise but the authors original collection contains many unmarked prints which I have tried to identify source but it is not easy at times.

Ian Clapperton. Plates 102, 215, and 223, **Alistair Douglas**. Plates 13, 76-81, 89, 91-99, 103-105, 107, 108, 112-116, 118. 126, 129-132, 149, 152, 163, 171, 173, 176, 178, 180, 183-193, 196-204, 206-209, 211-214, 216-222, 232, 233, 238, 239, 242-245, 249-252, 255, 258-260, and 263-266, **Robert Grieves**. Photos on pages 1-3 and plates 10, 27, 85, 86, 120, 158, 224, 226, 261, and 262, **Douglas Parker**. Plates 2, 3, 15, and 16-20, **Bob Parr**. Plate 136, **R. H. G. Simpson**. Plates 1, 5, 6, 7, 9, 22-26, 31-33, 36-41, 43-52, 53-75, 82-84, 87, 88, 90, 100, 101, 106, 109-111, 117, 119, 121, 122-125, 127, 128, 133-135, 137-148, 150-151, 153-157, 159-162, 164-170, 172, 174, 175, 177, 179, 181, 182, 194, 195, 205, 210, 225, 227, 231, 235-237, 240, 241, 246-248, 253, 254, 256, and 257, **Peter Walton Collection.** Plates 4, 21, 34, 35, 42, 228, and 234, **Brian Wright**. Plates 14, 28-30, and C1

Afterword.

Whilst this book will, as a single volume, interest those with particular memories of the 1961-85 era, the two volumes published to date are intended to be used as a set as some information carries over from the first book.

It was felt that in this series of books that complete fleet lists were inappropriate as that information is available elsewhere, however it is the intention of the Alexanders Study Group to provide this information in due course, at least for the pre 1961 period. Shortage of space has prevented the inclusion of a complete list of services operated in say 1985.

The Alexanders Study Group.

Has been formed to bring together all those interested in Alexanders buses and the products of Alexander Coachbuilders. Details can be obtained from the publisher by writing or phoning the address on the contents page 2, of this book. A quality bulletin is published occasionally.

Future Plans.

The first two volumes have covered the Alexanders story from 1945-85, and a third, on which work is advancing well, will cover the products of the Coachbuilding concern from 1945-60. In the fullness of time we intend to cover the whole of the Scottish Group of bus companies, concentrating on the 1945-85 period initially, but a book on Alexanders before 1945 has not been ruled out. We are always pleased to hear from readers who may be able to help with photographs for forthcoming books.